W9-BBE-369

ETHNIC CHRONOLOGY SERIES
NUMBER 7

The British in America
1578-1970

A Chronology & Fact Book

Compiled and edited by

Howard B. Furer

1972
OCEANA PUBLICATIONS, INC.
DOBBS FERRY, NEW YORK

Library of Congress Cataloging in Publication Data

Furer, Howard B   1934-
    The British in America, 1578-1970.

    (Ethnic chronology series, no.7)
    SUMMARY: A chronology of the British in the United
States from the sixteenth century to the present
accompanied by contemporary documents.
    Bibliography: p.
    1. British in the United States--History.
[1. British in the United States--History] I. Title.
II. Series.
E184 .B7F87   973*.04*21   72-8683
ISBN 0-379-00507-7

TABLE OF CONTENTS

To summarize in detail the total influence of British immigration to the United States in a short book such as this, is an almost impossible task. For it to be done properly, a rewriting of the first two centuries of American history would have to be undertaken, since the roots and origins of the United States lie principally in Britain, at least to the extent that British stock formed, by far, the largest element in the thirteen colonies by the time of the Revolution. However, with independence, the children and grandchildren of these early colonists became American, and the new arrivals from the homeland entered as immigrants.

In a very real sense, the history of British immigration to America is actually the story of four separate groups of newcomers; the English, Scotch-Irish, Scotch, and Welsh. Each group came to the United States and implanted its culture, and traditions upon this "New World." Two other groups, the Irish, and Canadians, could logically be included within the greater confines of the term British-Americans. However, because their experiences in the United States are different, and in many ways distinct, they have not been included within this study, and are mentioned only when they are part of the larger picture of the British immigrant experience.

Obviously, this volume is a cursory examination of an immigrant group that has been barely noticed by historians except for their importance to colonial American history. One can read whole volumes on the history of American immigration without finding more than a dozen or so references to those people who emigrated to America from the United Kingdom. Perhaps the reason for this neglect is the fact that the British immigrant experience is so complex and detailed, that students of immigration history do not wish to attempt researches into this perplexing problem. On the other hand, it may very well be that the British were here for such a long time, and in such great numbers that they are simply taken for granted; that is, they are rarely looked at as immigrants at all. Apart from bare immigration and census statistics, neither newspaper editors, official commissions, nor other contemporary writers mentioned these peoples of British origins.

In any case, it is the purpose of this study to cast as much light as possible, within the confines set by the publishers, on the total British immigrant experience. Whether the British were different or much the same as other ethnic groups that came to the United States, their history, by itself, is quite meaningful in the growth of the American Republic.

The problems in writing this work have been many; selection of pertinent data, lack of adequate and especially recent bibliographies on the subject, and a dearth of contemporary documents, to mention but a few of the difficulties. Nevertheless, this volume does accomplish its intended purpose; that is, it acts as a valuable and, in many respects, a comprehensive starting point for those students interested in pursuing the study of British immigration to and in the United States still further.

Howard B. Furer
Newark State College
Union, New Jersey

vi

CHRONOLOGY

British Immigration During the Colonial Period
1578-1799

1578

June 11   Sir Humphrey Gilbert obtained a patent from Queen Elizabeth I for discovery and colonization in northwest America. He made a voyage to the New World, but his plan to establish a colony had to await financial support.

1583

June   With five ships and 260 men, Gilbert reached Newfoundland, and made exploratory trips, but his vessel was lost on the homeward journey and no colony was planted.

1584

April 27   Sir Walter Raleigh, a half-brother of Gilbert was granted a virtual renewal of the Gilbert patent, and equipped an expedition under the command of Ralph Lane and Richard Grenville, which landed on Roanoke Island, and explored Albermarle Sound on the North Carolina coast.

1585

April 9   Raleigh named his discovery Virginia, and dispatched a colonizing expedition under Lane and Grenville, which landed on Roanoke Island. Grenville left Lane in charge of this first English settlement in America, but the colony was abandoned in June as a result of Indian troubles and Spanish tensions.

1587

May 8   An expedition under John White, an English painter, arrived at Roanoke Island on July 22, but found no survivors of the original colony. White left a group of colonists and sailed for home to obtain supplies.

August 18   Virginia Dare, the grandchild of John White, was born on Roanoke Island. She was the first English child born in the present United States.

1

1590

August 17   John White finally returned to the Roanoke Island settle-
               ment, but found no trace of the settlers. Their where-
               abouts has remained one of the great mysteries of Ameri-
               can history.

1606

August   James I gave the Plymouth Company rights to settle be-
               tween the 38th and 45th parallels in America.

1607

May 24   The London Company dispatched three vessels which reach-
               ed Virginia and disembarked at Jamestown. During the
               first seven months, famine and disease cut the number of
               settlers from the original 105 to 32, as councilors chosen
               before sailing proved unable to cope with the situation.

August 14   The first expedition of the Plymouth Company built a tem-
               porary fort at the mouth of the Kennebec River in New
               England, but this English colony proved unsuccessful.

September   Captain John Smith was elected President of the council
               governing Jamestown. His reforms marked a turning
               point for the colony as great emphasis was placed upon a
               self-sustaining agricultural community.

1608

August   Separatists from the Church of England (henceforth called
               Pilgrims) moved to Holland to avoid persecution. They
               came from Scrooby, Nottinghamshire. On May 1, 1609,
               they settled in Leyden.

1609

October   John Smith left Jamestown, and Thomas Lord De La Warr
               assumed authority. Dissension and lack of food marked
               this period in the colony's history, known as the "starving-
               time."

1611

May 23   Sir Thomas Dale assumed control of the Jamestown colony,
               and imposed severe penalties to check internal disorder.
               Many constructive developments occurred under his rule,
               as well as that of Thomas Gates, Dale's successor.

1612

John Rolfe, one of the English colonists at Jamestown, introduced tobacco cultivation in the settlement, and this proved to be an excellent crop for export. Rolfe later married the Indian princess Pocohantas.

1619

The Virginia Company transported shiploads of maidens to Jamestown in order to provide wives for the early male settlers, and create a larger population.

June 19
Leaders of the Leyden group of Pilgrims, including John Robinson and William Brewster, set up a joint stock company with a Virginia Company patent in the name of John Wyncop to settle near Jamestown.

August 9-
14
The first colonial legislature in the New World, the House of Burgesses, met at Jamestown. Sir Edwin Sandys, who had gained control of the London Company, and George Yeardley, the newly appointed Governor of Virginia were primarily responsible for the introduction of this reform, as well as others.

1620

July 9
Pilgrims under William Brewster left Holland for England in the ship Speedwell.

July 22
The Pilgrims joined other English Separatists and non-Pilgrims in Plymouth and set out for America on the Speedwell and the Mayflower. The Speedwell sprang a leak and returned to port.

September 16
The entire company of Englishmen crowded aboard the Mayflower and sailed for the New World. Myles Standish served as military leader. The ship carried 101 persons, including 14 indentured servants and hired artisans. There were 35 from Leyden, and 66 from London and Southhampton.

November 9
The Mayflower entered Cape Cod Bay, far north of its original destination.

November 21
Since the patent from the Virginia Company was inoperative in the North, and since they were afraid the non-Pilgrims would rebel, the Pilgrims persuaded 41 adults a-

board to sign the Mayflower Compact. The signers agreed to follow laws for the "general good of the colony."

December 26   The Mayflower anchored at Plymouth, and the settlers went ashore to establish their colony.

1621

April   Deacon John Carver, the first governor of Plymouth, died, and was succeeded by William Bradford, who held that office, with the exception of five years, down to 1656. Over half of the settlers died of disease during the first winter.

June 1   The Plymouth Company was reorganized by the Council for New England, and received a patent to settle at Plymouth in America.

1622

August 10   The Council for New England granted Sir Ferdinando Gorges and John Mason the land between the Merrimack and the Kennebec Rivers.

1623

Beginning in 1623, British settlers began arriving at Great Bay, New Hampshire, including Portsmouth, and at the Saco River and Casco River in Maine. Among the leaders of these groups were David Thomson, Christopher Levett, John Oldham, and Richard Vines.

1623

March   The Pilgrims at Plymouth colony granted each family of settlers a parcel of land.

1624

The Dorchester Company planted a colony of Dorsetshiremen on Cape Ann. Proving ill-suited to both fishing and agriculture, most of the settlers returned to England.

April   English settlers were among the 30 families that settled New Netherland, at Governor's Island, on the Delaware, and at Fort Nassau.

May 24

The London Company went into receivership, and was placed under the management of the Privy Council. Its charter for Virginia was revoked, and Virginia became a Royal Colony.

August 24

Sir Francis Wyatt, who was appointed the new Governor of Virginia was instructed to convene the House of Burgesses "once a year or oftener."

1626

Forty Dorsetshire settlers under Roger Conant moved to Salem, north of Boston, where they established a trading post.

November 15

The Plymouth Company in London sold all rights to the settlers, who divided up the remaining land. Eight pilgrims, including William Bradford, took over the debts of the colony. The Corporation and the colony were merged, but Plymouth never received a royal charter.

1628

September 6

The New England Company received a patent from the Council for New England for land from three miles south of the Charles River to three miles north of the Merrimack River, and it sent 40 settlers to Salem.

1629

New Hampshire and Maine were divided at the Piscataqua River, Gorges receiving all the land north of the River, and Mason all the land to its south.

March 14

The Massachusetts Bay Company, successor to the New England Company, received a royal charter which specified no location for its annual meeting. This oversight made it possible to transfer the government to New England and transform the company into a self-governing commonwealth.

April

The Massachusetts Bay Company dispatched its first fleet to America with settlers, who landed at Salem.

August 26

The Cambridge Agreement came about when religious and economic difficulties led John Winthrop, Richard Saltonstall, and others of the Massachusetts Bay Company, most of them Puritans, to decide to migrate to the New World

provided the charter and the government of the company
went with them. The company agreed, and Winthrop was
elected governor.

1630

March 29

Beginning in March and carrying through to November,
more than 1,000 English settlers sailed for Salem in 17
ships, and then founded Boston, Charlestown, and Water-
town. The 12 freemen (company stockholders eligible to
vote) consisting of the governor, deputy governor, and
assistants ruled the colony.

1631

Lords Say and Seele and others received a patent from the
crown for Connecticut.

May 28

The number of freemen in Massachusetts Bay was raised
from 12 to 130, but only churchmembers could be freemen.
The governor was still elected by the assistants, who were
chosen by the freemen. Direct election of the governor
by all freemen began in 1632.

December

Ferdinando Gorges received a grant of 24,000 acres on the
Agamentieus River, and began focusing his colonizing activity in that area.

1632

June 30

George Calvert, first Lord Baltimore, succeeded in induc-
ing King Charles I to grant him territory north of the Po-
tomac River. The Maryland charter was granted after
his death. His son, Cecelius Calvert, second Lord Baltimore, was recognized as proprietor of the county Palatine
of Durham.

1633

The elevation of William Laud to Primate of England, com-
bined with increasing economic difficulties led to an influx of new settlers into Massachusetts Bay including such
notable clergymen as John Cotton and Thomas Hooker.

1634

Each town in the Massachusetts Bay colony gained the
right to send deputies to the meeting of the General Court,
which passed all laws for the colony.

February 27   The first group of Maryland settlers arrived. Some 200 English emigrants, including two Jesuits and many other Catholics were in this party. They settled at a place called St. Mary's.

1635

September 13   Reverend Roger Williams was banished from Massachusetts Bay for preaching his belief in the separation of church and state.

October   Connecticut patent holders sent John Winthrop Jr. to settle at Saybrook, at the mouth of the Connecticut River.

1636

A representative system of government began in Plymouth. The General Court consisted of two deputies from each town, together with the governor and his assistants.

May 31   Settlers from Massachusetts Bay established Withersfield, and in the same year, Hartford, under the leadership of the Reverend Thomas Hooker.

June   Roger Williams and his followers founded the relatively democratic colony of Providence, Rhode Island.

1637

May   Settlers from Hartford, Windsor, and Withersfield founded what became the colony of Connecticut with a representative General Court for the population of 800.

May 27   John Winthrop was reelected Governor of Massachusetts Bay, and continued to serve in that office almost every year to 1649.

July   Reverend John Davenport and a merchant, Theophilus Eaton, founded the colony of New Haven, Connecticut.

November 17   The Antinomion views of Anne Hutchinson, John Wheelwright and others threatened Puritan orthodoxy in Massachusetts Bay. Antinomions stressed personal revelation, denied that Christians had to follow moral law, and questioned the power of the orthodox clergy. Anne Hutchinson was banished from the colony.

1638

| April | Anne Hutchinson, after her expulsion from Massachusetts Bay, settled Portsmouth, Rhode Island. |

1639

| January 24 | Hartford, Withersfield and Windsor agreed to the fundamental Orders, which called for the governor and magistrates to be elected by "admitted inhabitants." |

| May 8 | William Coddington founded Newport, Rhode Island, and a year later Newport and Portsmouth were united. |

1640

By 1640, some 20,000 Englishmen had emigrated to New England for a variety of causes.

A large group of English immigrants arrived in Maryland. The majority were Protestant, and immediately disliked the strong position Catholics held in the colony.

1641

| December | The Body of Liberties made Massachusetts Bay a commonwealth or independent republic dominated by the church. |

1642

Sir William Berkeley, Governor of Virginia, introduced a number of reforms, including the abolition of the poll tax. He also forced the Indians to cede all lands between the York and James Rivers from the falls to Kecoughton.

1646

| November | Reverend John Eliot began to convert the Indians in Eastern Massachusetts to Christianity. By 1663, he had translated the Bible into the Indian language. |

1647

| May 31 | Providence, Newport and Portsmouth formed the British colony of Rhode Island. The Governor and both houses of the legislature were elected annually by the freeholders. |

1649

January 30   Virginia announced its allegiance to the Stuart house after
                  the execution of Charles I, and gave refuge to prominent
                  English Cavaliers who emigrated to America.

April 21   During the administration of William Stone, a Protestant,
                  as deputy Governor, a Toleration Act was passed in Mary-
                  land. The Calverts, Catholics, recognizing the fact that
                  Protestants outnumbered Catholics in their proprietor-
                  ship, and wishing to safeguard the religious liberty of
                  the Catholic settlers, agreed to this statute.

1652

A few dozen Scottish Royalist and Covenanter prisoners
were transported to Virginia after the Battle of Dunbar.

1653

English settlers from Virginia began moving into the Albermarle Sound region in what was later North Carolina.

1656

July   English Quakers began arriving in Massachusetts Bay.
                  Two of them were banished from the colony, however, be-
                  cause of religious non-conformity.

1657

The earliest immigrant society founded in America was
the Scot's Charitable Society of Boston.

1658

October 27   Massachusetts Bay established the death penalty for ban-
                  ished Quakers who returned. In 1658, William Robinson
                  and Marmaduke Stevenson (Quakers) were hanged by or-
                  ders of the General Court.

1660

With the Restoration of the Stuarts, the Virginia colony
embarked on hard times between 1660 and 1675. The Navigation Acts, declining tobacco prices, the Dutch Wars, a
cattle epidemic, servant uprisings and the reintroduction
of the poll tax all caused conditions to deteriorate.

1661

The proprietary regime in Maryland became increasingly unpopular as a result of the decline in Tobacco prices, the restriction of the suffrage to freeholders, Indian raids, absentee proprietorship, official nepotism, and continued anti-Catholic sentiment.

1662

English colonists from New England arrived at Cape Fear to raise cattle, but left in 1663.

November   Connecticut requested from the crown and received a charter granting it autonomy under the Fundamental Orders, and allowing it to absorb New Haven.

1663

April 3   Charles II granted land in the Carolinas between the 31st and 36th latitudes to eight proprietors including Sir Anthony Ashley Cooper. Proprietors had the power of government with the consent of the freemen, and religious liberty was to be granted.

July 18   Charles II granted Rhode Island a charter, but allowed it to continue under its independent rule. A statement was added about religious toleration, and Rhode Island continued to operate under this document until 1842.

1664

July 4   The Duke of York granted John Lord Berkeley, and Sir George Carteret, land between the Delaware and Hudson Rivers. Their "Concessions and Agreements" (1665) provided for a governor appointed by the proprietors, a council appointed by the governor, an elective assembly, and religious freedom. Governor Philip Carteret brought about 30 English colonists to Elizabethtown in 1665.

September 7   The English, under Colonel Richard Nicolls, captured New Netherland from the Dutch, and renamed it New York. By this time, the English inhabitants already outnumbered the Dutch residents of the colony.

1669

March 11   The Fundamental Constitutions of the Carolinas, calling for aristocratic government was issued. It never went into effect.

May   Massachusetts Bay colony annexed Maine.

                                        1674

                             Lord Berkeley sold his interest in New Jersey to two
                             English Quakers, who later turned the land over to four
                             Quaker trustees, including William Penn.

                                        1676

May 10   Nathaniel Bacon, a recent British immigrant, led a force
                             of frontiersmen who demanded reforms in the Virginia
                             colony.   Bacon's Rebellion, as this incident is known, last-
                             ed for several months until Bacon died suddenly in October.
                             His followers were caught, and 23 of them were hanged.

July 11   The colony of New Jersey was divided into East Jersey
                             under Carteret, and West Jersey under the Quakers.

September   A short-lived uprising under William Davyes and John
                             Pati occurred in the Maryland proprietorship.   It was
                             crushed and the two leaders were hanged.

                                        1677

March 13   The Lords of Trade upheld the title to Maine of the heirs
                             of Ferdinando Gorges.   Through its agent, John Usher,
                             Massachusetts proceeded to buy out the heirs of Gorges
                             for 1,250 pounds.   Maine remained incorporated in Massa-
                             chusetts until 1820.

                                        1679

                             After the Battle of Bothwell Brig, several dozen Scottish
                             Royalist and Covenanter prisoners were transported to
                             Virginia by the English government.

                                        1680

September   New Hampshire became a separate Royal Province, and in
                             1692 was detached from the Dominion of New England.
                             However, from 1698 to 1741, New Hampshire shared a gov-
                             ernor with Massachusetts, gatting its own chief executive,
                             Benning Wentworth, in 1741.

                                        1681

March 14   Charles II granted to William Penn, land in America be-

tween the 40th and 43rd latitudes.   Penn intended his colony
to be a haven for persecuted English Quakers, but advertised widely for colonists.   Although British immigrants
formed the largest segment of the population, large numbers of Germans also settled in Pennsylvania.

1682

The first Welsh settlement in America was established near
Philadelphia.   It was a supposedly autonomous region
known as the "Welsh Tract."

1683

Another group of Welsh immigrants acquired a tract of
land of some 40,000 acres.   This area was known for two
generations as the "Welsh Barony."

Several hundred Scots were brought to settle Perth Amboy
by the Scottish proprietors of East Jersey.   The larger
Scottish movement would take place later on in the eighteenth century, for Scotland, as a foreign country, was de-
barred from British colonial trade, and Scots had therefore little opportunity to reach America.

October   A Scottish colony under Henry Erskine was founded at Port
Royal, South Carolina, but was overrun by the Spanish in
1686.

1684

A small group of Scots were brought to America by the
proprietors of the Carolinas to settle Stuart's Town in
southern Carolina.

1689

February 13   William and Mary ascended the English throne.   Reforms
were introduced in Virginia, and many grievances were
redressed.   The reforms prompted new emigrations from
England to America.

1691

October 17   Massachusetts became a Royal Colony with a governor
appointed by the crown, with property rather than religion as a qualification for voting, and with a royal veto
power over all legislation.   In the same year Massachusetts annexed the Plymouth colony.

1692

English settlers brought many of their superstitions with
them to America. When Salem, Massachusetts girls pre-
tended to be bewitched, Governor William Phips, under
clerical influence, set up a special court to try those
accused of witchcraft. The colony executed 20 and im-
prisoned 150.

1699

By 1699, several Welsh settlements had been established in
Pennsylvania. They included Guynnoyd, Bryn Mawr, Mer-
ion, Haverford, and Radnor.

1700

By 1700, there were already a dozen Presbyterian churches
in the colonies, primarily of Scotch and Scotch-Irish origins.

1702

April   The crown united the two Jerseys into one royal province.
The colony shared a governor with New York until 1738,
when Lewis Morris was appointed the first Governor of
New Jersey.

1706

The first American presbytery was organized in Philadelphia, largely through the efforts of a Scotsman, Francis
Makemie.

1707

The Act of Union between England and Scotland took place,
and this began a new era in Scottish emigration. Taking
full advantage of their newly acquired opportunities, numerous Scots settled as merchants and factors in colonial
seaports, and a steady stream of Lowland artisans and
laborers left Glasgow to become indentured servants in
the tobacco colonies and in New York.

1714

Between 1714 and 1720, fifty four vessels carrying Scotch-
Irish emigrants docked in New England, and even more

entered harbors in the South. Western Massachusetts, Maine, and New Hampshire soon had Scotch-Irish settlements, while New York's Orange and Ulster Counties still reflect the origins of these settlers. In fact, the single largest group of eighteenth century newcomers were the Scotch-Irish. About 250,000 of them came to America in half century or so before the American Revolution.

March   Scotch-Irish immigrants began coming to Pennsylvania, and many moved south down the Valley of Virginia.

1715

Because of their role in the Jacobite Rebellion of 1715, several score Scottish Highlanders were transported to the American colonies by the British government.

1716

Crop failures in the northern counties of Ireland prompted many Scotch-Irish to emigrate to America. These Ulster Scots carried with them to the New World a deep hostility toward England which was inbred in succeeding generations.

1717

The number of convicted British felons who came to America increased considerably, when an act of Parliament created the new legal punishment of transportation, and contractors began to take out regular shipments from the English jails.

May   Large scale departures of Scotch-Irish to America took place as a result of the termination of leases in Ulster, which had been granted on easy terms 30 years earlier in an attempt to attract Protestant settlers to Northern Ireland.

1718

The Scotch-Irish were not particularly welcomed in New England, where they were regarded as "the blockish Presbyterians from a barbarous nook of Ireland."

April   A small Scotch-Irish settlement was begun in Maine. It was later absorbed by the town of Portland.

June   James Logan, the provincial secretary of Pennsylvania,
                            settled the frontier township of Donegal with Scotch-Irish
                            who seemed to have a special penchant for frontier living
                            and Indian fighting.

                                        1719

                            Londonderry, New Hampshire was settled by about 20
                            Scotch-Irish families. The site was selected by James
                            McKean, the grandfather of the first president of Bowdoin
                            College.

                            Samuel Waldo imported Scotch-Irish settlers to Maine,
                            and one little settlement in that colony was named Cork.

                                        1720

                            By 1720, there were several hundred Scotch-Irish families
                            settled along the Kennebec River, and in Eastern Maine.

March   Scotch-Irish settlers established a frontier community at
                            Worchester, Massachusetts.

July   The inhabitants of the Scotch-Irish settlement of London-
                            derry, New Hampshire, protested against being called Irish,
                            and insisted that their chief loyalty was to the British
                            crown.

                                        1725

                            The bulk of the Scotch-Irish emigrants headed for the
                            colony of Pennsylvania, because of the unfriendliness they
                            found in New England, and because most of the vessels
                            leaving Belfast and Londonderry for America, were en-
                            gaged in the flax-seed trade, of which Philadelphia was the
                            leading colonial center.

                            Scotch-Irish servants had a bad reputation for crime and
                            violence, which shocked staid New Englanders, and
                            caused nativist feeling toward these newcomers.

                                        1726

                            The Welsh were regarded as desireable immigrants.
                            Maryland tried to attract Welsh farmers into that colony
                            by granting special exemptions in land and taxes.

1727

A heavy wave of Scotch-Irish emigration to America set in, and although reports to the British government attributed it primarily to the evils of the land system, and a succession of bad harvests in the northern counties of Ireland, a variety of other causes were cited.

March

Hugh Boulter, Archbishop of Armagh, and Lord Primate of all Ireland, estimated that fewer than one in ten of the Scotch-Irish emigrants had money enough to pay their passage to America.

1729

Ship captains sent agents to markets and fairs in Ulster to gather Scotch-Irish emigrants, and assure them of good land in America. By such methods, and others, great numbers of Scotch-Irish were induced to go to the colonies, many of them as indentured servants.

Several Scotch-Irish settlements were established in South Carolina by Governor John Johnson with the expressed purpose of guarding the frontier. They were also to be used to help put down any Negro slave uprisings in the colony.

July

A mob of nativist Yankees in Boston, showing their dislike for the Scotch-Irish, arose to prevent the landing of a ship carrying Scotch-Irish emigrants.

1730

Welsh immigration, which was never very large during the colonial period, virtually stopped altogether when Wales adopted a more tolerant attitude toward Welsh Friends. (Quakers)

February

The Scotch, St. Andrew's Society of Charleston, South Carolina was organized.

1732

South Carolina granted twenty square miles of land to a group of Scotch-Irish immigrants from Ulster County, who arrived in the colony early in the year.

May	Several shiploads of Scotch-Irish emigrants from Belfast settled Williamsburg Township on the Santee River in South Carolina.
June 20	James Ogelthorpe and others received a grant of land between the Altamaha and Savannah Rivers, named Georgia. Ogelthorpe sought a refuge for English convicts, especially debtors.

1733

While Lowland Scots generally came to America individually, most immigrants from the Scottish Highlands arrived as members of organized groups. Lachlan Campbell of Islay received a large grant of land from Governor William Cosby of New York, and brought several hundred Highlanders, who had been tenants of his in Scotland, to settle near Lake George.

February 12   Savannah, Georgia was founded by Ogelthorpe, who brought with him to America several hundred English debtors and convicts. He ruled as a benevolent despot with no assembly.

1734

Welsh immigrants found employment in the slate quarries along the lower Susquehanna River.

At Worchester, Massachusetts, a Yankee mob destroyed the newly built Scotch-Irish Presbyterian church in another display of early nativism.

Londonderry, New Hampshire had a Scotch-Irish population of 700, and offshoots of this settlement had already been established in Rockingham, Hillsboro, and Merrimack Counties.

1735

May   A Highland Scottish group from Inverness, established a settlement along the frontier on the Altamaha River in Georgia.

1736

A Scotch-Irish settlement was founded in Duplin County, North Carolina.

By the fall of 1736, a considerable direct movement from Ulster to South Carolina was taking place, as Scotch-Irish immigrants came to this Southern colony in response to the encouragement of immigration by the provincial authorities.

1737

The son of a Cornish immigrant acquired the great Cornwall iron deposit in Pennsylvania.

1738

March

Thirty four Scotch-Irish families encountered so much resentment from their English neighbors in Worcester, Massachusetts, that they moved farther west, and established a community at Pelham, Massachusetts.

June

In Virginia, largely because of the heavy Scotch-Irish influx, the colonial assembly created two new counties in the valley, Frederick and Augusta Counties.

1741

Blandford, Massachusetts was settled by a group of Scotch-Irish immigrants.

1743

Mutual antagonism of the Scotch-Irish and the Germans produced so many disturbances in Pennsylvania, especially at election time, that the Penn family instructed their agents to sell no more land to Scotch-Irish immigrants in the predominantly German counties of Lancaster and York, and to offer those Scotch-Irish already there generous terms to move to the Cumberland Valley.

1745

A number of Scottish Highlanders, who had taken part in the Jacobite Rebellion of 1745, were transported to the American colonies.

The first county lieutenant of Augusta County, Virginia was a Scotch-Irishman, James Patton.

Scotch-Irish Presbyterians took part in the emotional religious movement of the 1740's knows as the Great Awakening.

1746

Princeton, the College of New Jersey, was Scotch-Irish Presbyterianism's most significant contribution to higher education in colonial America. Jonathan Dickinson was its first president, and the Reverend Aaron Burr, its second.

1752

July 4

Georgia became a Royal Colony with an assembly. The bulk of the population, by this time, were English indentured servants.

1758

The Scotch-Irish Presbyterian Synods of New York and Philadelphia united. Princeton became the authorized training school for Presbyterian ministers.

1759

The Scotch-Irish chartered a company for the relief of minister's widows and children. It was probably the first insurance company in the United States.

1760

By 1760, New Jersey had an important Scotch-Irish element; these people settled in the back-country areas of the colony. Most of them had originally come as indentured servants, and were Presbyterian.

1763

The movement of Scottish Highlanders to America gained momentum. Poverty, crop failures, cattle blights, and suffering, along with higher rents and the eviction of crofters from their holdings to make way for sheep runs, all acted as causes for emigration. Many went to the Mohawk Valley, as well as the upper reaches of the Hudson. Many other thousands, encouraged by the liberal inducements offered by the North Carolina legislature, settled in the Cape Fear region. Differing as they did from the rest of the colonial population in language, dress, and social customs, the Highlanders found adjustment much more difficult than their Lowland countrymen.

1764

December 13-
27

A group of Scotch-Irish in back country Pennsylvania, known as the "Paxton Boys," marched on Philadelphia to demand the redress of grievances that they suffered along the frontier, the most important of which was the failure of the Quaker oligarchy in the colony to protect the frontier against Indian attacks. Benjamin Franklin persuaded them to disperse and return to their homes.

1765

Between 1765 and 1776, some 25,000 Scots migrated in family groups to the colonies. The roads in Scotland were filled with young and old alike, bound for America.

April

Sir William Johnson, an Ulster man belonging to an English family, settled a group of 400 Scotch Highlanders on his crown grant of 100,000 acres along the Mohawk River, near Gloversville, New York. The Highlanders came from the clan MacDonnell.

1767

The Scotch-Irish frontier had reached Uniontown, Pennsylvania.

November

David Caldwell, a Scotch-Irish minister started a classical school near Greensboro, North Carolina, and ambitiously called it, "the Eton of the South." Other institutions in which Scotch-Irish Presbyterians have been influential are Allegheny College, Waynesburg College, Geneva College, and Westminster College, all in Pennsylvania.

1768

Dr. John Witherspoon, who came to America from Scotland in 1768, became president of Princeton, and gave the little college its national reputation.

1769

Between 1769 and 1774, 44,000 Scotch-Irish in 152 different ships came to America. Most of them were in their twenties. While Pennsylvania received the largest share of the influx, New Jersey and Maryland began to seem equally inviting. Like the Germans, many Scotch-Irish trekked down the valley from Pennsylvania, settling in the back country of the Southern colonies.

1771

May 16   In back country North Carolina, the Scotch-Irish formed the bulk of the Regulator Movement, which struggled against eastern political dominance, and the oppressions and extortions of the Tidewater officials. The Regulators, however, were crushed by colonial troops at the Battle of Alamance. Many of these Scotch-Irish Regulators became Tories during the American Revolution.

May 17   James Few, one of the Scotch-Irish Regulator leaders was executed on the battlefield at Alamance by North Carolina Governor, William Tryon.

1773

Scottish Lowland immigration reached its peak, when a trade depression, and a substantial rise in rents induced many weavers and farmers to seek better opportunities in the American colonies.

1774

The Highlanders who had settled along the Mohawk River, strongly attached themselves to the interests of Sir William Johnson, and when he died in 1774, they transferred their allegiance to his son, Sir John Johnson.

More than 10,000 Scotch-Irish emigrants were leaving Northern Ireland annually, especially as a consequence of a depression in the linen trade, and the development of an acute agrarian crisis.

1775

As late as 1775, ninety-eight percent of the population of the New England colonies was of English stock.

Scotch-Irish schoolmasters were quite numerous in the colonies, especially in Pennsylvania as of 1775.

In Boston, a number of Scotch-Irish remained loyal to the British government, and formed a body called the Loyal Irish Volunteers to oppose the American rebels.

Several Scotch-Irish Regulator counties sent a number of addresses of loyalty to the Royal Governor of North Carolina at the outset of the American Revolution.

A group of 200 Highland Scots left Scotland from the port of Greenock. They found homes in upper New York, and in North Carolina.

May   Thirty Scottish families met at Killin in Perthshire. Dressed in the Highland fashion, they marched to Greenock, where they boarded a ship to America.

1776

By 1776, approximately 250,000 to 300,000 Scotch-Irish had come to the American colonies.

By the eve of the Revolution, there were about 150,000 Scotch-Irish living in Pennsylvania. They comprised one-third of this colony's total population. A majority of the assembly, however, was still English Quaker.

Scotch-Irish communities were scattered throughout the colonies. Nearly 70 were in New England, from 40 to 50 in New York, from 50 to 60 in New Jersey more than 130 in Pennsylvania, about 100 in Virginia, Maryland and Tennessee, 50 in North Carolina, and about 70 in South Carolina and Georgia. A zone of Scotch-Irish Presbyterian churches extended from the New England frontier to Georgia, for the advance of the Scotch-Irish pioneers was everywhere marked by the establishment of small Presbyterian churches.

Charleston, South Carolina ranked second only to Philadelphia as a port of disembarkation for Scotch-Irish emigrants.

At the time of the American Revolution, the population of the New England colonies as a whole, was preponderantly of English origin, while in the middle colonies, the English were the largest element comprising about fifty percent of the total population. In the South, there were large German, Scotch-Irish and Negro minorities to modify the predominantly English character of the region.

Nearly all the Scotch-Irish in Pennsylvania supported the American Revolution, many of them becoming ardent and agressive patriots. To the Pennsylvania Radical Whig party, they supplied a large proportion of the rank and file, and such leaders as George Bryan, Thomas McKean, and Joseph Reed. They also contributed the majority of the officers and men of the military unit known as the "Pennsylvania Line."

In the back country of the Carolinas, the Scotch-Irish were most sharply divided on the issue of the American Revolution. Those in North Carolina, if not outright loyalists, were at least extremely hostile to the Revolutionary cause. In western, South Carolina, there were many loyal Scotch-Irish, especially in the isolated frontier settlement known as Ninety-Six. In this region, however, there were some Ulstermen, like Alexander Chesney, who fought for both sides in turn. On the other hand, in the Waxhaws----the back country borderland between North and South Carolina----the British found the Scotch-Irish universally patriot.

The nearest approach to unanimity among British immigrants at the time of the American Revolution could be found among the Scots. While a number of individuals of Scottish birth, like John Witherspoon, James Wilson, Arthur St. Clair, and John Paul Jones, served the cause of the Revolution, most Scots were almost solidly loyalist.

February 27   In Cumberland County, North Carolina, a formidable force of Highland Scot loyalists was raised, only to be crushed at the Battle of Moore's Creek Bridge.

July 4   Two of the signers of the Declaration of Independence were English-born; Robert Morris and Button Guinnett. All of the others, with one exception, were of British origins.

November   Many Scottish merchants, especially in Virginia, joined the loyalist side. They warmly welcomed Lord Dunmore's arrival in Norfolk, and hastened to join the "Queen's Own Loyal Virginians."

1777

The Continental Congress sent two Presbyterian ministers to persuade the Scotch-Irish of back country North Carolina to support the Americans in the Revolution. This effort produced a meager response.

July   Scotch-Irish in New England took part in the campaign against the southward march of General John Burgoyne's troops.

August 16   A striking indication of the disunity among the Scotch-Irish in the American Revolution was the fact that while the New Hampshire Scotch-Irishman John Stark rose to become a Revolutionary General, and the victor at the

Battle of Bennington, his brother William Stark fell at Long Island while serving as a Colonel in the British Army.

1778

The Scotch-Irish in Pennsylvania were not a solid patriot bloc. Sir Henry Clinton succeeded in forming in Philadelphia a loyalist regiment known as the Volunteers of Ireland, made up of a considerable number of Scotch-Irishmen, most of them deserters from the Continental Army.

November 11   Many Scottish Highlanders of the Mohawk Valley served under Sir John Johnson in Butler's Rangers, participating in the Cherry Valley Massacre; after the war, they formed the vanguard of the loyalist migration to Canada.

1780

The Philadelphia Scotch-Irishman, George Bryan was the author of the Pennsylvania statute of 1780 abolishing slavery in the state. Yet, the measure was vehemently opposed by the back-country Scotch-Irish, who, at the same time, loudly demanded freedom for themselves.

October 7   North Carolina Scottish Highlanders fought on the British side at the Battle of King's Mountain.

1781

January 1   The Scotch-Irish "Pennsylvania Line" mutinied at Morristown, New Jersey as a result of the ill treatment of the "Line" by the Pennsylvania Assembly. At the same time, they rejected inducements to desert, offered to them by the British Army.

1783

April   Immigrant ships bearing Scotch-Irish reached the Delaware, even before the ink on the Treaty of Paris was dry. Within a year or two, the Scotch-Irish movement regained all its former regularity, and the Scotch-Irish again formed the most numerous group of newcomers to America. As before, most of them were indentured servants.

November   Three Scottish brothers built the first cold blast furnace in Franklin County, Pennsylvania.

1788

The British government passed an act which forbad the emigration of skilled artisans from the North of Ireland, thereby curtailing, somewhat, Scotch-Irish emigration.

1789

The first General Assembly of the Presbyterian Church in America convened in Philadelphia. Its leadership was furnished by Scotch and Scotch-Irish Presbyterian ministers, such as William Homes, Thomas Craighead, Joseph Smith, Matthew Henderson, John McMillan, and Thaddeus Dodd.

The British Consul at Philadelphia, Phineas Bond, reported that well over 20,000 Scotch-Irish immigrants had come to Pennsylvania since the end of the Revolutionary War, and that the influx showed no signs of slackening.

1790

The Census reported that the state of Massachusetts had a Scotch population of 13,435.

December 20   The Englishman, Samuel Slater, who arrived in America in 1789, carrying in his head the plans of the spinning jenny, established the first American cotton factory at Pawtucket, Rhode Island. Slater was only one of a great number of British artisans whose skills were a vital element in the initial phase of American industrialization.

1791

Alexander Hamilton sent agents to Scotland to engage framesmiths, stocking weavers, and other Scottish artisans for work at the Society for Useful Manufacturer's National Manufactory at Paterson, New Jersey.

1793

John and Arthur Scholfield arrived in America. They built woolen mill machinery from memory, and started their own factory at Byfield for a group of Massachusetts capitalists.

Joseph Gales, a British journalist, who became editor of the Raleigh Register, and the official reporter of Congres-

sional debates, fled to America to avoid arrest for criti-
cizing the British government, who had severely curtailed
freedom of expression and assembly after the outbreak of
war with revolutionary France.

May

A British ship, <u>Sisters</u>, carrying a large group of British
emigrants was intercepted in mid-Atlantic by a French
privateer. They informed the French that they were
leaving England because they opposed the war against
France, and they were then allowed to continue their voyage to America.

1794

Morgan John Rhys, a Welsh clergyman, fled to the United
States. He purchased 25,000 acres of land in Cambria
County, Pennsylvania, where he founded a colony, which,
during the next few years, attracted a steady stream of newcomers from Wales.

Dr. Joseph Priestly, the noted British liberal clergyman
and scientist, and Thomas Cooper, emigrated to the United
States. They and their friends sought sanctuary in a congenial fellowship to be established along the Susquehanna
River in Pennsylvania. But, Priestly and his fellow in-
tellectuals were unfitted for the rigors of frontier living,
and their settlement failed to prosper.

July

The Scotch-Irish of Fayette and Westmoreland Counties
in Pennsylvania, played a leading role in the Whiskey
Rebellion which was crushed by the administration of
George Washington.

1798

A mass exodus of Welsh took place. It had been originally projected to settle on the extensive lands owned by
the Pulteney family in western New York State. With
the failure of this overly ambitious enterprise, plans more
limited in scope were drawn up and successfully carried
out with immigrants going to both New York and Pennsylvania.

It was generally conceded that the Scotch-Irish loved their
whiskey, and the vice of consuming too much of it occas-
sionally extended upward in the social scale, even as far
as the clergy. In 1798, the town meeting of Londonderry,
New Hampshire voted to restrict the sale of liquor at fairs
because they had become something of a nuisance.

1800

Scotch Presbyterianism formed the backbone of the fanatical religious outburst in Eastern Kentucky known as the Great Revival of 1800. It was sponsored by James McGready and John McGee.

The Scotch-Irish frontier settlements in Pennsylvania extended to the western-most limits of the state. Many of these Scotch-Irish frontiersmen were known as "Donegallians."

By 1800, the majority of the early teachers of music in the United States were of English background, and, thus, the early musical life of eastern cities was an offspring of English conditions. The English music teachers were the first to bring the music of the German masters before the American public, while English singers and English operettas were quite popular with many Americans.

Visitors to the textile mills of New England and the middle Atlantic states constantly remarked upon the prominence of Englishmen and Scots, whose function it was to superintend and instruct native Americans in new manufacturing techniques.

Small groups of Welsh immigrants cooperated in their settlements at Utica, New York, in Cambria County, Pennsylvania, and at Paddy's Run (Shandon) in Ohio. The success of these pioneers induced hesitant countrymen in Wales to seek their fortunes overseas.

December 3   The Scotch-Irish as a group supported Jeffersonian Republican principles, and vehemently opposed the Federalists. In the presidential election, they cast their votes solidly for Thomas Jefferson.

1801

The Welsh Baptist Church in Utica was organized, and the only appreciable immigration into Oneida County in New York State was Welsh.

1802

A Welsh Congregational Church was established in Utica. During the Peace of Amiens signed with Napoleon Bonaparte by the English government, emigration from the British Isles to America spurted upward for a brief period of time.

1803

The British Passenger Act of 1803 drastically reduced the numbers that immigrant ships were allowed to carry, and for all intents and purposes, killed the trade in Scotch-Irish indentured servants. Scotch-Irish immigration to America, never again amounted to anything like it has been during the eighteenth century.

1806

From a single glen in the Scottish Highlands, twelve whole families emigrated to America. Since families in Scotland meant all the blood relations, this movement almost depopulated this entire area in the Highland region.

1808

A Pittsburgh company with English equipment and workmen started the first flint glass furnace in Pennsylvania.

1810

Although Scotch-Irish emigration had come to a virtual standstill, there were enough Scoteh-Irish living in Pittsburgh to make it the most Scotch-Irish city in the United States, with its strict observance of the Sabbath, and its Calvinistic blessing on material prosperity.

In Radnor, and St. David's, Pennsylvania, Welsh was used in the church services and legal documents, although most of the early Welsh settlements in that state had been fully Anglicized by 1810.

1812

Some 7,500 British aliens registered at the outbreak of the War of 1812. More than 1,600 registered themselves as farmers, planters or gardeners. One thousand of these newcomers listed themselves as textile workers or makers of textile machinery. Another 800 were merchants, clerks and bookkeepers, 700 were building trades workers, and some 3,000 were industrial laborers.

An Englishman constructed and operated the first iron rolling mill in Pittsburgh, using primarily British workers.

The Scotch-Irish moved westward with each stage of the frontier and by 1812, Ohio had its Scotch-Irish settlements at Aberdeen, Edinburgh, and Caledonia.

1814

At Utica, New York, the Ancient Britons Benevolent Society was founded by several Welsh immigrants.

1815

In the fall of 1815, unexpectedly large numbers of farmers from England and the Scotch Highlands debarked from ships tying up at the wharves of Philadelphia and New York. They had come across in both cabin and steerage quarters.

The first American manufacturer of Brussels or Wilton carpets, hired Scottish workers from Kidderminster for his Philadelphia mill.

Not all British emigrants after the War of 1812 were headed for the United States. Canada became the destination of a considerable number, particularly small farmers of substance, who were attracted to the upper provinces, where they found not only fertile land, but also a government and society like that at home.

1816

December 4

The first man of Scotch-Irish origins to be elected President of the United States was James Monroe. Others elected in later years include, Andrew Jackson, James K. Polk, James Buchanan, William McKinley, and Woodrow Wilson.

1817

The Welshman, Thomas Cotton Lewis, erected the first American mill for puddling and rolling bar iron, and afterward build several more in Pennsylvania and Ohio.

Many of the farmers leaving England, were coming to America with sums ranging from 200 to 2,000 pounds.

Although the British exodus included a great number of unskilled workers from the towns and cities, the majority of British immigrants during the ante-bellum years probably consisted of farmers and agricultural laborers. Some of the farmers possessed large amounts of capital, such as Morris Birkbeck, who, in 1817, sold his property in Surrey, and emigrated with a capital of 18,000 pounds, and a quantity of prize livestock to Illinois, where he hoped to establish an English colony.

1819

The Panic of 1819, cast a shadow over British immigration that lasted for several years. Newcomers arriving in the panic year, in ignorance of the economic setback, beseiged the British consulate for aid.

1820

The first breweries in Cincinnati, contrary to popular belief, were begun by Scotch and English brewers of ale, not German brewmasters.

1821

William Hall, a small farmer in England, gave these reasons for leaving Britain in 1821; 1-) the difficulty of providing for his large family, 2-) to escape oppression, misery, hypocricy and tyranny, 3-) the hope of civil and religious liberty in America, 4-) no prospect of amelioration in England, 5-) the prospect of pointing out the same road to distressed friends and relatives.

April

Passage money was supplied by American employers for many English calico printers, who were urged to bring their machinery with them to the United States.

1822

The first British-American newspaper to be printed in the United States was the Albion, published in New York. It lasted until 1876. Others, such as the Old Countryman (1829-1848), the Scottish Patriot (1840-1842), and the Anglo-American (1843-1847), reprinted news from the latest British papers to reach New York by packet ship.

1825

When the British Parliament repealed the ban on the departure of artisans, Lowell, Massachusetts textile mill-owners, secured Manchester experts to work in their factories.

Robert Owen, a Scottish Utopian Socialist, established a communitarian colony at New Harmony, Indiana.

1826

An emigration society composed of unemployed Scottish weavers appealed successfully to public benevolence for the means to finance their members' departure to the United States.

March

The House of Commons appointed a select committee, headed by Wilmot Horton, to encourage emigration from the United Kingdom.

1827

In the coal fields of eastern Pennsylvania, the bulk of the miners were of British origins. First came the English and Cornish, later followed by hundreds of Welsh colliers.

The first sixteen miners from England to work in the Pennsylvania coal fields were imported by a Pottsville, Pennsylvania coal company.

April 9

Three hundred persons from Scotland left Great Britain for New York. They were among the better class of Scottish mechanics.

1828

The Connecticut carpet making village of Thompsonville, to which Kilmarnock workers flocked, became virtually a Scottish town.

American employers paid the passage of many British calico printers from Liverpool, and encouraged British operatives to bring British machinery with them.

By 1828, some 10,000 Welsh per year were leaving the United Kingdom for the United States.

James Smorielie, a Scotsman from Edinburgh, who came to the United States in 1828, found employment as an engraver of bank notes. From this occupation, he progressed to become one of the Nation's leading engravers of landscapes.

1829

By 1829, more than 4,000 English miners had settled in the Pennsylvania coalfield areas.

In Lowell, Massachusetts, weavers and overseers from Paisley, Scotland, established the in-grain carpet industry.

Mine owners in eastern Pennsylvania were so pleased with Welsh immigrant miners, that they sent home two Welsh preachers to induce more miners to leave Wales and come to the United States.

1830

From 1830 on, Welsh colliers were in great demand. Mine owners in Carbondale, Pennsylvania offered to pay the passage of Welsh mining families to the United States. By the end of the year, twenty Welsh families had arrived in Carbondale.

Thousands of British immigrants migrated to the New England states, where they found jobs as ordinary mill hands.

Beginning in 1830, and proceeding for the next 20 years, hundreds of Cornish immigrants migrated into the lead mining region of southwestern Wisconsin.

1831

The British government established the Government Commission on Emigration for the purpose of collecting and diffusing information concerning the United States to prospective emigrants.

Cyrus MacCormick, a Scot, invented the reaping machine. There have been so many Scottish-Americans who have contributed to the field of invention in the United States, that it would be impossible to list them all here; a random sampling would include, Samuel F. B. Morse (telegraph), Joseph Henry (telegraph), Peter Cooper (locomotive), and James Scott and George Lauder (steel industry techniques.)

1832

A Welsh weekly journal, the first of its kind in the United States, began to be published. It was entitled Cymro America, and was printed in New York City.

At Cincinnati, two Englishmen, William and John Garrard, began to produce the first fine crucible steel in the United States.

Chamber's Edinburgh Journal began to be published, containing articles on emigration for the information of prospective British emigrants. It had a very large circulation reaching its intended audience of farm laborers, servants, and artisans.

1833

A survey done in 1833, showed that the mining population of America's coal regions was almost exclusively composed of English and Welsh miners, with a few Scotchmen.

1834

A former English immigrant from Liverpool, brought 600 of his countrymen, who were white-ware (pottery) workers, to his factory in Troy, Indiana. However, within a few years, this enterprise proved a failure.

The changes in the English Poor Laws were directly responsible for the emigration of scores of small farmers and tenant farmers to the United States.

The Poor Law Amendment Act of 1834, authorized parishes in Britain to mortgage the rates in order to subsidize emigration, although the Act also stipulated that those assisted were, in the future, to be sent to a British colony and not the United States.

1835

Philadelphia became a center of woolens production, and attracted thousands of British woolen mill operatives.

William Firmstone, an English mill manager, constructed
a series of hot-blast furnaces in Ohio, Pennsylvania, and
Kentucky, and became a leading pigiron manufacturer in
the United States.

1836

The Highland Society of New York, held its "First Sport-
ive Meeting." Within the next thirty years, Scots in
Boston, Philadelphia, and several other cities, likewise
staged Highland games.

James Taylor, an English immigrant, founded the Trenton,
New Jersey pottery works.

1837

The first Mormon overseas mission was founded in London.
Several others were established during the next few years.

Edward Nock, an Englishman, who in Wales had learned
the boiling method of "puddling", introduced this technique
into the iron factories of Pittsburgh.

In Richmond, Virginia, there were enough Welshmen employed at the Tredegar Forge and Rolling Mills, to hold a
rousing St. David's Day Celebration.

An agent for a Lowell mill in Massachusetts, recruiting in
England, found that sixty persons from the old English town
of Uley were about to emigrate. He persuaded half of
them to come to his mill. In subsequent years, others from
the West Country followed them to Lowell.

1839

A Pennsylvania company hired a Welsh ironworks superintendent, David Thomas, who had mastered the hot-blast
process in Scotland, to set up the first successful furnace
of this type in America.

New England's one great Welsh community sprang up on
the Vermont-New York line, when granite quarrying began in that area.

By 1839, there were 46 Welsh churches in America, of
which 16 were Congregational, 13 Baptist, 12 Calvinistic

Methodist, 3 Wesleyan Methodist, and 2 Episcopalian.
By 1872, the total number of Welsh churches had risen
to 384.

1840

American banknote makers imported English copperplate
printers under the contract labor system.

Robert Lennox, founder of the Presbyterian Hospital, and
the Lennox Library in New York, was a Scottish immigrant,
who was considered one of the five wealthiest New Yorkers
before his death in 1840.

By 1840, English and Scottish textile operatives had supplanted the famous American mill girls of Lowell, and
dominated New England's textile factories.

Davis Thomas' hot-blast furnaces had become an unquali-
fied success. As a result of his contribution, he became
known as the father of the American iron industry.

When Queen Victoria married, the British of New York
celebrated for two days, regaling several hundred poor
English, Scottish and Irish widows of the city with a roast
ox, and a thousand pound wedding cake.

Beginning in 1840, English cutlers came to America to work
in Pittsburgh, Bridgeport and Waterbury, Connecticut.
These skilled workers were highly prized by American
manufacturers who induced many of these specialists to
emigrate with the promise of high wages.

In Britain, the Colonial Land and Emigration Commissions
were established to combat fraud and misrepresentation
perpetrated upon departing British emigrants to the United
States. It published substantial pamphlets called Colonization Circulars containing valuable information on the
New World.

Up to 1840, the early labor movement in the United States
was led by English and Scotch immigrants. While the Britons continued to play an important role in labor organization, after 1840, many new German immigrants also took
the lead in labor activities.

Emigration from England began on a large scale, and coin-
cides with the changes wrought by the establishment of the
modern factory city.

October

As a result of the activities of the Mormon missionaries
in England, a sizable migration of British Saints to America began in the fall of 1840.

1841

While most of the Welsh emigration was from the rural
regions in Wales during the depression of 1841, urban
departures from Wales rivaled rural emigration in numbers and intensity.

James Bennett, an immigrant Derbyshire potter, discover-
ed a large and suitable clay deposit along the banks of the
Ohio River, and with his three brothers built the first East
Liverpool kiln in America.

Robert Clarke, a Scotsman, who had been brought to Cincinnati by his immigrant parents, became a pioneer in
American printing and publishing in the mid-west.

1842

A group of unemployed Staffordshire potters appealed to
the British government for funds to finance the departure
of a number of its group to the United States.   The government complied, and hundreds of these potters emigrated.

Due to economic depression in Great Britain, emigration to
America became the primary topic of conversation.   However, because of a lack of funds, hundreds of jobless Englishmen could not leave the Old Country and were forced
to return to their villages and towns where the depression
was at its worst.

1843

January 18

A Welsh Society was formed in New York City for social
and benevolent purposes, to preserve the purity of the
Welsh language, to celebrate Welsh national holidays, and
to protect Welsh immigrants from fraud and exploitation.

February 15

Three Welsh magazines began to be published in New York
State.   They contained stories of the Old Country, illus-
trations,   and feature articles of Welsh happenings in
America.

1844

In Philadelphia, anti-Catholic rioters included a considerable Scotch-Irish Presbyterian element. These riots were part of the general nativist upsurge of the pre-Civil War years.

1845

Beginning in 1845, and extending for the next 45 years, Cornish immigrants had their American hey-day in the copper and iron mines of Michigan.

Skilled Welsh quarrymen from Blaenau Ffestiniog, directed by their countrymen, who had leased likely sites, were exploiting the Peach Bottom slates of York, Lancaster and Harford Counties in Pennsylvania.

A former English blacksmith, Benjamin Haywood, built the country's first rolls for making "T" rails, and the first apparatus for sawing hot iron.

1846

Welsh farmers, who were having difficulty eking out a living from the soil in Maine, began a small slate industry in that state, which proved quite successful.

When the Wamsutta Textile Mill in New Bedford, Massachusetts opened, the majority of its employees were English immigrants.

1847

A Scottish Robert Burns Club sprang up in New York City, the first of its kind in America. Dozens soon followed in other cities.

1848

Textile mill-owners in Holyoke, Massachusetts, imported two or three hundred Scotswomen with training as weavers to work in their factories.

By 1848, Staffordshire potters who emigrated to the United States, went almost invariably to East Liverpool, Ohio or, Trenton, New Jersey, while Welsh quarrymen could be found migrating into the slate regions of Vermont, New York and Pennsylvania.

The British miners of Pennsylvania were sending home thousands of dollars annually or using their savings to bring their families to America to join them.

Andrew Carnegie, who was to become the leader in the steel industry in the United States, came to America with his poverty stricken parents from Dunfermline, Scotland.

1849

Several large groups of Welsh immigrants participated in the California gold rush.

The Englishman, John Bates, with Welsh and English assistants, organized the first union in the Pennsylvania anthracite coal fields.

A military company of Scotch-Highlanders was formed in New York by the Sons of Fair Caledonia.

December 10   The Caledonian Club of Albany, New York celebrated St. Andrew's Day with a parade and a gala ball.

1850

Unlike German or Scandinavian farmers in the mid-west, the English and Scots seldom huddled in communities of their own kind. The Welsh, on the other hand, did huddle together in their own group colonies.

When the Maryland soft coal miners struck-----many of them Scots-----they secured a former Lanarkshire union leader, William Clachan, to guide them in their struggle.

By 1850, New York City had a number of immigrant military companies of Scotch and Scotch-Irish origins. They included the Highland Guards, the Scottish Guards, and the Caledonian Fusiliers.

Duncan Phyfe, a Scotch immigrant came to America, and began building the tables, chairs, and secretaries that have made him the patron saint of antique dealers.

By 1850, there were about 7,000 people of Cornish origins in southwestern Wisconsin, and the language used by the older inhabitants in this district, even as late as 1930, gave evidence of a persistent Welsh influence.

In 1850, the largest number of miners in the Wisconsin and Illinois lead regions, and the copper and iron mines of Michigan, were of Cornish origins.

1851

The British Women's Emigration Society was organized in London. It was a private philanthropic agency, whose primary purpose was to aid emigrating British females.

Many British urban workers took up land in America rather than seek new employment in the American cities. At Canton, Illinois, many of the English farmers in that area, had been textile hands in Lancashire.

1852

The first Scottish Caledonian Club in the United States was organized at Boston.

154

In 1854, a peak year for immigration, 59,000 immigrants from Great Britain arrived in the United States.

A Scotch-Irish Protestant Mutual Relief Society was organized in Boston.

1855

A government survey indicated that the workingmen in the new iron centers of the middle-west were chiefly Welsh immigrants.

1856

Many Welsh dreamed of founding a purely Welsh settlement in America-----Trefedigaeth Gymreig-----where they could live under the ancient laws of Hywel Dda. One such colony, which a Llanbrynmain group under Samuel Roberts started in Eastern Tennessee, soon foundered because of poor soil and the outbreak of the Civil War.

157

The Welsh community in Oneida County, New York, im-

ported Humphrey R. Jones, a famous Welsh preacher from
Wisconsin, to conduct revival services in their settlement.

The Scottish-American Journal, owned and edited by
Archibald M. Stewart was founded. It was the leading
Scottish newspaper in America until it ceased operations in
1919. Other leading Scotch newspapers were, the Scotsman (1869-1886), the Boston Scotsman (1869-1886), the
Boston Scotsman (1906-1914), and the Caledonian (1901-
1923).

A colony of Scottish miners from Wanlockhead was established in and around Pittston, Pennsylvania.

1858

The Cornishman, Richard Esterbrook, organized his steel
pen company in Philadelphia, and brought English artisans
from Birmingham to work in his factory.

Joseph Hartley, an unemployed Yorkshireman left England
for the quarries of upstate New York. He reported that
there were plenty of "Jhan Beels" to meet him. And, there
were, indeed, many Welsh and English working in the quarries of New York, Vermont and Pennsylvania, comprising
the single largest ethnic group engaged in this occupation.

159

Calvert Vaux, one of the two designers of New York's Central Park, was an English landscape gardner who emigrated
to the United States.

1860

On the eve of the Civil War, more than 750,000 immigrants
from the United Kingdom had arrived in the United States.
This figure accounted for one ninth of all arrivals in America between 1815-1860.

By 1860, there were about 55,000 emigrants from England
alone living in the trans-Mississippi West. The Welsh
were the next largest group, with about 38,000 in this region.

By the end of 1860, more than 30,000 Mormons from Great
Britain had emigrated to the United States, most of them
going to the Great Salt Lake Valley in Utah.

By 1860, English immigrants were working in the more intricate crafts of the woolen industry, while ordinary operatives were mostly native Americans.

June
The first Welsh Eisteddfod west of the Rocky Mountains was held by Welsh gold miners in North San Juan, California.

1861

The British Amalgamated Society of Engineers set up its first American branch, which was to become an important professional organization in the United States during future years.

In Southwestern Illinois, two Staffordshire miners, Daniel Weaver, and Thomas Lloyd, united the bituminous colliers into the nucleus of a national union, the American Miners' Association. John Hinchcliffe, an English tailor turned American lawyer, became its president, and held that post until the Union's demise in 1868.

April
A big Scottish festival, with bagpipes, reels, kilts, and quoits, was held in New York City for the benefit of the 79th regiment, the "Highland Regiment," that went off to the Civil War with uniforms patterned after those of the "Black Watch."

September 26
The Association of Welsh Congregational Churches of New York was formed. It included twenty-two different Welsh churches.

1862

During the Civil War, an agent recruiting soldiers for the North with false promises of jobs, inveigled Aston glass-blowers to emigrate to America.

1863

During the Lancashire "cotton famine," brought on by the Civil War in the United States, unemployed British operatives clamored for assistance so that they could emigrate, while the American labor shortage led northern manufacturers to recruit hands in Scotland and England.

August 20
The Scotch soldiers of the "Highland Regiment" proved to be excellent fighters, but they were intractable and undisci-

plined, and as a result, 37 of them were arrested for
mutiny and desertion.

1864

A government survey showed that most British immigrants
who arrived in the United States in this year had a particular skilled trade, and came with specific jobs in mind.

1865

The Welsh Musical Union was organized among Welsh
farmers and miners in Wisconsin for the purpose of holding annual musical conventions, and offering prizes for
musical compositions.

By the end of the Civil War, nearly the entire English silk
industry had emigrated to the United States.

1866

From 1866 to 1885, the Census began to count persons
entering the United States from British North America.
More than 895,000 persons entered the country by coming across the border during this period, and undoubted-
ly the proportion of British-Americans among them was
very high although statistics are not available.

From Great Britain, a sizeable outflow took place as a
result of industrial depression. Lancashire textile workers, Yorkshire woolen operatives, and Macclesfield silkworkers were among those who came to the United States
in 1866.

Thousands of colliers from Staffordshire, Durham, and
Scotland, arrived to work in the bituminous coal mines
west of the Allegheny Mountains.

1867

John Player, an English pig-iron manufacturer, introduced his improved hot-blast stove at West Conshohocken,
Pennsylvania.

The Scottish Grand National Curling Club of the United
States was organized. Nearly every Scottish settlement
in the northern states had its own curling club.

The most numerous group of British industrial emigrants
to arrive in the United States in 1867, were coal miners
from Durham, Scotland and Wales, and iron puddlers and
rollers from the Black Country, who began leaving the
Old Country as a result of industrial depression.

The British Amalgamated Society of Carpenters and Join-
ers set up its first American Branch.

Welsh emigrants on board ships bringing them to America,
wrote home about the predominance of tea, coffee, and hard
biscuit in their diet, as well as potatoes, "stinking" codfish,
the need to buy food from the crew at inflated prices, the
steward's filthy hands, and the cramped quarters where
emigrants had to eat alone.

1868

Several British immigrants were pillars of the National
Labor Union of the 1860's; John Hinchcliffe, Richard F.
Trevellick, and Andrew C. Cameron among them. The
majority of the rank and file were also of British origins.

John Siney organized the Workingmen's Benevolent Association, known after 1870 as the Miner's and Laborer's
Benevolent Association. Siney, a Lancashire Irishman,
led English, Welsh and German colliers.

1869

The Amoskeag Mill of Manchester, New Hampshire, imported fifty Scottish girls skilled at weaving fancy ginghams.

Three Scottish immigrants who came to Quincy, Massachusetts, introduced granite polishing machinery to the United
States granite industry.

With unemployment, wage cuts, and strikes throughout
Lancashire, British trade unions helped hundreds of their
members to emigrate, while thousands more pressed to
follow the few fortunate ones.

English miners opened a tunnel under Broadway in New
York City. Old Country skill at rock tunneling had many
uses in the United States.

The American Emigrant Aid Society of London, conducted a lottery, the winning prize being the passage money to San Francisco.

1870

In Cincinnati, Samuel Danks from the Black Country, devised a long desired mechanical puddler which, though puddling itself was becoming outmoded, attracted the entire American iron industry's attention. The invention also stirred up considerable British interest.

George West, once a Devonshire paper worker, became the greatest paper manufacturer in the United States.

The Pennsylvania Railroad, and several western lines including the Sante Fe, opened a London agency to sell cheap and comfortable passage to the American West, and to help immigrants select farms.

A London charitable society financed the emigration of several dozen English families to West Virginia, where employment was found in the coal mines.

Dr. Edmund Duncan Montgomery came to the United States from Scotland. He settled in Texas, where he wrote The Vitality and Organization of Protoplasm, a massive and important work in the medical field.

A band of 300 Sussex emigrants settled in Geary County, Kansas, and during the early 1870's, English farmers settled whole villages in that state. As a rule, however, as earlier, only a few British herded together.

By 1870, the English, Scots, and Welsh together, made up about fourteen percent of the total foreign-born population of the United States.

Surveys showed that by 1870, most iron works and steel mills in the United States relied upon Scots and Welshmen for their working forces.

Edward Edginton, an English immigrant, worked for the Iowa State Emigration Board, and placed advertisements in a number of British newspapers, and agricultural publications, propagandizing the opportunities in that state.

A group of Welsh immigrants organized the Cambrian Mutual Aid Society in San Francisco.

By 1870, many of the Welsh in the Wisconsin lead mining region had abandoned their original occupation to become farmers and successful stockbreeders.

Welsh immigrants comprised almost eighty percent of the workers in the American slate industry.

In 1870, the Welsh in Boston, New York, Philadelphia and San Francisco held Eisteddfod celebrations, highlighted by parades of all of their social and benevolent societies.

February 21   The Welsh community in Boston displayed a very festive mood in a special observance of St. David's Day, featuring a parade, and a ball.

1871

Thousands of Cornish miners were working in the silver mines of Nevada, and the iron deposits in the Lake Superior district in Wisconsin and Minnesota.

Between 1871 and 1896, more than 3,000,000 emigrants from the United Kingdom left their homes to go to the cities, mines, and mill towns of the American West.

July   A group of Scottish immigrants established a colony in western Minnesota for the purpose of raising pure bred cattle.

1872

The Burlington and Missouri Railroad organized a colony of English farmers in Iowa. One hundred and forty five settlers were brought over from England.

British soft coal miners in America were working sixty to a hundred hours a week for $2.65 a day.

August 17   Politically, the Welsh have generally been Republican, and the Y Drych, the oldest Welsh newspaper in the United States, supported the party even during the schism of 1872.

August 20   Many British-American labor leaders supported the National Labor Reform Party in the presidential election of 1872. Andrew Cameron was secretary of that party's national convention.

1873

The Panic of 1873 considerably slowed down emigration from the British Isles to the United States. However, within a few years, the tempo of the British movement once again picked up.

Princeton, the original "Presbyterian College", with a Scottish president, held its first "Caledonian Games," with a Scottish athlete from Montreal , George Goldie, as gymnastics instructor.

Several hundred Somerset, Devon, and Yorkshire farmers and artisans took up eight townships of Northern Pacific Railroad and homestead land in Clay County, Minnesota, and gave their colony the name Yeovil.

A Scottish silk merchant from London, planted the Victoria colony of Kansas on 70,000 acres of land purchased from the Kansas Pacific Railroad. Despite its prosperity, the colony broke up in the mid-1880's.

A Welsh Presbyterian church was organized in San Francisco. It was the first of its kind in that city.

1874

The Furness Colony in Wadena County, Minnesota, was planted on 42,000 acres of railroad land by a tightly knit group of several hundred prosperous North of England farmers and tradesmen.

Welsh immigrants began pouring into Kansas in such large numbers that the Santa Fe Railroad had to put on special trains to bring them into that state.

1875

The great Fall River, Massachusetts textile strike was largely a Lancashire immigrant affair. It was inspired, led, and participated in by hundreds of English textile workers.

The Burlington Railroad published a monthly newspaper, "The Iowa and Nebraska Farmer," which was sent to Great Britain in an effort to attract British immigrants to lands held by the railroad in Iowa, Nebraska and elsewhere in the West.

Andrew Carnegie's superintendent at the Braddock, Pennsylvania steel mill, was the son of a Welsh immigrant ironworker. American manufacturers disliked skilled British worker's wage demands no less than their conservatism.

June

The various English societies and organizations in the United States and Canada, federated in the North American St. George's Union, and held annual conventions during the next three decades.

1876

Beginning in 1876 and lasting for the next four years, 15,000 British farmers emigrated to the United States. They scattered throughout the states and territories of the West.

The American Land Company of London advertised a hundred thousand acres of land in southwest Minnesota, while the Land Colonization and Banking Company of London offered 20,000 acres of land complete with town sites and grain elevators in Minnesota and Iowa. Similar companies brought British farmers to Kansas, Oregon and the Dakotas.

A steel company brought English workmen to its new Tennessee iron town of South Pittsburgh, and Scottish capitalists hired Scottish foremen to start mills in Tuscarawas County, Ohio. However, both of these ventures failed.

February 14

Alexander Graham Bell, a Scotsman, invented the telephone. Other Scots who have distinguished themselves as American engineers and inventors were James Laurie, James Pugh Kirkwood, and Peter Campbill the "dean of the linoleum industry."

1877

The Granite Cutters Union, with their many Scottish and English members, was the first important labor organization to adopt strike benefits. However, British-born labor leaders were usually conservative in their tactics, and had little use for extremists.

James Braidwood, a Scottish pit boss in Illinois, introduced the "long wall" system of mining in place of the "room and pillar" method. This new technique was soon being used all over the United States.

August   In Pittsburgh, a number of Welsh citizens organized a
                      colonization society to aid their countrymen in emigrating
                      from the crowded Eastern industrial sections of America
                      to the more rural West.

                      1878

                      In a meeting in Boston, a group of Scots organized the
                      Order of Scottish Clans, the most famous and influential
                      of all British ethnic societies.

                      1879

                      With the depression of the early 1870's over, good times
                      returning to the United States, and the British economy
                      touching bottom, a massive flow of emigration to America
                      began again.

                      The North Wales Miner's Association offered seven pounds
                      to any member who would go to America. They also urged
                      unemployed members to leave the country and start a new
                      life in the United States.

                      Texas disappointed English farmers, when several land
                      companies, who were urging them to emigrate, offered
                      land that was not only poor for farming, but also for graz-
                      ing cattle.

                      A corps of English bookmakers monopolized the straight
                      betting business at the Saratoga racetrack in upper New
                      York State.

                      British immigrant farmers were paying $25 an acre for
                      land in New Jersey, or what was usually paid as annual
                      rent in England.

                      Le Mars, Iowa was begun by three brothers from Cam-
                      bridge, England. Hundreds of young, upper-class English-
                      men took up farms in the area, and a gracious community
                      was established. However, within a few years, Le Mars
                      lost its distinctiveness.

                      The year 1879 saw the last great flood of British iron and
                      steel workers coming to the United States. Thereafter,
                      this group of emigrants was negligible.

October 3   Seven hundred and fifty woolen mill workers from York-
                      shire, organized as a group, emigrated to the United
                      States to find better jobs.

1880

By 1880, the primary causes for British emigration to the United States were economic. Advertising, "American Letters," charitable or friendly aid were all secondary motivations.

Thomas Hughes established a colony of English immigrants at Rugby, Tennessee. The settlement never really prospered, and by 1896, because of the sterile soil there, it collapsed completely.

In 1880, 6,000 Englishmen were employed in the Philadelphia carpet works, the largest single foreign-born group so engaged.

Boom times in the United States, brought scores of Welsh slate workers to Bangor and Penargyle, Maine.

Most of the 1,300 American members of the Power Loom Brussels Carpet Weavers Mutual Defense and Benefit Association were of English birth or ancestry.

Richard Trevellick, a Cornish immigrant, who had been active in labor activities in the United States for twenty years, became the most outstanding labor leader in the mining industry.

By 1880, southern Massachusetts was drawing the bulk of the incoming English immigrants, who found jobs in the rapidly growing textile industry of that area.

A Welsh literary journal, but printed in English, the Cambrian began its existence in Cincinnati, and later appeared fortnightly at Utica, New York. It suspended operations in 1919.

A newspaper, The American Settler, published in London, portrayed the advantages of life in Western America. It contained letters of successful emigrants to inspire the hesitant, and was published until 1892.

November 2   James A. Garfield was elected twentieth President of the United States. His ancestor was Edward Garfield, a Welshman, who had come to America in 1630.

1881

Between 1881 and 1885, nearly 18,000 British farmers emigrated to the United States. Most of them went to the states of the West.

Samuel Gompers, a London cigarmaker, arrived in the United States in 1863. After a successful career in labor organization he became the main figure in the organization and establishment of the Federation of Organized Trades and Labor Unions of the United States and Canada, which was reorganized in 1886 as the American Federation of Labor. Gompers became its first president, a post he held until his death in 1924.

By 1881, the leading Welsh communities in Ohio were in Jackson County; at Radnor in Delaware County; and in the "Welsh Hills" of Licking County, near Newark, Ohio.

Welsh choral societies gave frequent concerts, not only in the various Welsh churches, but also in a number of large concert halls in different cities across the nation.

December 1   In Cincinnati, the Caledonian Club staged a rather large St. Andrew's Day celebration, replete with bands, athletic contests, parades, and formal dinners.

1882

The year 1882 was another peak year for immigration. It saw a total of 103,000 immigrants from Great Britain arrive in the United States. Never again, would British immigration to America approach that figure.

1883

British immigration to the United States dropped to a little more than 76,000 persons.

At the height of the Northern Pacific Railroad's colonization campaign, that railroad employed throughout the United Kingdom more than 800 agents to recruit emigrants at town markets and country fairs.

Scottish immigrant workers at Fall River, Massachusetts, turned out the first high quality gingham ever produced in the United States.

1884

The census reported the arrival of 65,950 immigrants from Great Britain. While many of these newcomers stayed in the eastern industrial centers, thousands of them migrated to the farming or cattle areas of the West. Vast tracts in Iowa, Minnesota, and other western states were bought up by these Britons. In thirty two different tracts, they owned an area equal to one-fourth of the British Isles. From Texas and New Mexico, north to Wyoming, British syndicates and private investors owned 20 million acres of rangeland. Several of the syndicates sent out British managers and herdsmen. The young Britisher took to cow punching as he never did to ploughing.

May

Descendents of the pre-Revolutionary Highland settlers of North Carolina, their towns still known as the "Scotch Settlements," welcomed 300 poor Scotch crofters, whom a wealthy benefactress had sent to America from Skye.

1885

British immigration to the United States dropped to a little more than 57,000 persons.

The United States Congress passed a law which forbad contract labor. This statute cut deeply into the numbers of British textile and mine workers who had been coming to the United States.

Chris Evans, Daniel McLaughlin, John Pollock, and John Jones, all British-born, became the leaders of the National Federation of Miners and Mine Laborers. In 1890, they helped to organize the United Mine Workers of America.

A New York bricklayer complained that seven or eight hundred English and Scottish competitors for jobs were arriving every year.

By 1885, in the woolen mills of western Massachusetts, Welsh operatives outnumbered every other nationality group employed in these factories.

The census estimated that 19,000 British farmers emigrated to the United States during the five year period beginning in 1885. After 1890, a rapid decline set in.

Traveling through Kansas, with two pairs of ferrets, one old Englishman exterminated prairie dogs at one cent a head, making his own distinctly British contribution to the American economy.

By 1885, the name of Fall River, Massachusetts, became synonomous with "America" among British immigrants going to that section of the United States.

1886

Among Samuel Gomper's aides in the formation of the American Federation of Labor were many other British immigrants, including John Jarrett, Robert Howard, William Martin, James Duncan, and Dan McLaughlin.

In London, the Emigrant's Information Office was established to provide all sorts of data to departing emigrant groups or individuals who were going to America. It survived until 1918.

1887

Two thousand Scottish stone masons landed in New York during six weeks of the Spring of 1887, overcrowding the labor market there for lack of rail fare to inland cities.

A few Scotsmen started playing golf in a vacant lot in Yonkers, New York, the first golf club in the United States being formed there under the august name of St. Andrew's.

To commemorate Queen Victoria's Jubilee in 1887, every town in America with enough British-Americans to form a committee, had its special church services, processions, outings, and banquets.

The Scotch Presbyterian Church of America was organized on a national basis. It held two Gaelic services each week.

The Welsh singing group of Pittsburgh won first prize in a National Welsh Eisteddfod, and the group representing Scranton took second place in the contest.

A party of unemployed English men and women, whom the Duke of Buckingham had sent to the United States in 1888 were deported under a law of 1882 which excluded immigrants likely to become public charges.

In 1888, the 3,755 underground workers of the Lehigh and Wilkes Barre Coal Company were 29 percent Welsh, 12 percent English, and 1 percent Scotch, representing almost half of the total miners employed by this company. Much the same pattern could be found in similar mining corporations.

1889

The Census of 1889 reported that there were nearly 2,000,000 people of British birth widely scattered throughout the United States. They could be found primarily in Michigan and Illinois, as well as other parts of the middle-west. Among this large group were 250,000 Scots and 100,000 Welsh.

Some British unions regularly helped unemployed members to emigrate. The British Cotton Spinner's Society gave an emigration benefit to members who were prominent in trade disputes, and had become so called "marked men" in the Old Country.

A number of mining towns in Illinois, Iowa and Missouri had large Welsh, Scottish and English populations. Braidwood, Illinois was Scotch, Bevier and Huntsville, Missouri were Welsh, and Hiteman, Iowa, English.

April — The Scotch-Irish Society of America was founded in Columbus, Tennessee.

September — The dearth of skilled glassblowers forced a manufacturer at Jeannette, Pennsylvania, to import 25 Englishmen skilled at that trade.

1890

In 1890, almost 70,000 people from Great Britain emigrated to the United States, bringing the total for the decade 1881 1890 to 644,680. However, 214,892 of these immigrants returned to their homelands by the turn of the century.

The Census reported that 70,000 British were in Illinois, 76,000 in Massachusetts, and 144,000 in New York, comprising 8,12 and 9 percent of the respective total populations of each of these states.

By 1890, there were 36,000 British in New York City, 28,000 in Chicago, and 11,000 in Boston.

Over half of the surviving 92,000 British-born farmers in the United States lived east of the Mississippi River. Many British did move west, but because of discouraging results in the western states, the greater majority took up older acres in the east for more congenial market gardening or dairying.

There were 2,000 British-born potters in the United States, comprising one seventh of the total workers in the entire industry.

Throughout the American glass industry, more than 2,000 British glassworkers constituted 22 percent of the foreign-born and 6 percent of the entire labor force.

Several thousand boot and shoemakers from England and Scotland worked in America, though many returned home as machines supplanted custom work.

In 1890, the 15,000 British-born workers in the primary iron and steel industry comprised one-tenth of all employees and a quarter of the foreign-born.

In all branches of the American stone industry, there were nearly 8,000 British immigrants, constituting 28 percent of the foreign-born or 13 percent of all. Nearly half of them were of Scottish birth.

Nearly a tenth of all machinists in the United States, and fully three tenths of the foreign -born were, at one time, immigrants from Great Britain.

Scores of Welsh miners began returning home, and while most British-American colliers stayed in the United States, new arrivals no longer kept their ranks full.

Some 2,453 persons from England, who described themselves as farmers, entered the United States.

In 1890, there were about 25 soccer clubs in Fall River, where 2,000 persons might turn out to see a game, Philadelphia had seven soccer clubs, composed entirely of British immigrants.

By 1890, it was discovered that British skilled workers tended to move to the same occupation in America, that they had practised in the Old Country. Cotton and woolen workers moved from the North of England to New England, miners from South Wales to Pennsylvania, granite workers from Aberdeenshire to Vermont, pottery workers from Staffordshire to Ohio, Cornish copper miners to copper, iron and lead deposits in Michigan and elsewhere.

Throughout the hosiery industry, more than one third of the foreign-born male operatives were British immigrants, while one third of the woolen operatives and one fifth of the cotton workers were from the British Isles.

Among English, Welsh, and Scottish immigrant workers listed by the Census of 1890, fully 48 percent of the men, and 42 percent of the women were engaged in industrial occupations.

By 1890, Slovak, Magyar, Polish and Italian miners began to replace the English, Scotch and Welsh miners in the Pennsylvania bituminous coalfields.

1891

Beginning in 1891, despite the fact that the United Kingdom was economically depressed, the number of British immigrants to the United States annually declined. In 1891, only 66,605 persons from the British Isles arrived in America.

Thomas Cook, and other British agencies were distributing folders for the Chicago, Milwaukee and St. Paul Railroad, advertising the opportunities in Illinois and Minnesota for prospective British immigrants.

1892

In North Carolina, the descendents of the colonial Highlanders had their corner of the state reorganized as "Scotland County."

In 1892, there were about 700 Welsh living in Osage County, Kansas, and more than 1,000 in the neighborhood of Emporia, with six churches holding services in Welsh in the former, and three in the latter.

In a reply to a questionaire sent to the governors of the various states by the Immigration Protection League, seven states expressed a desire for English and Scotch immigrants above all other groups.

1893

By 1893, about 15,000 British silk workers from Macclesfield had emigrated to Paterson, New Jersey, whose silk
industry flourished during the 1880's and 1890's.

The American Protective Association movement was especially strong among the Scotch-Irish, who were very anti-
Catholic in their views.

1894

Welsh immigrants formed the bulk of the miners and
managers of over half the collieries in the state of Washington.

1895

Only 28,833 persons from the British Isles came to the
United States. In addition a strong return current after
1895, reduced the British-born population of the country.

In Cambridge, Massachusetts, a group of Prince Edward
Islanders organized the unique American congregation of
MacDonaldites, a sect peculiar to their province, and mod-
estly named it "the Church of Scotland."

1896

British immigration kept dropping, as only a little more
than 24,000 Britons arrived in the United States.

January 25   Scottish-Americans, wherever they lived in the United
States, honored their great poet, Robert Burns, in 1896 to
commemorate the hundreth anniversary of his death.

1897

A Cymradorian Society was organized in California among
the Welsh to encourage music, literature, and good fellowship.

The Daughters of Scotia, a social and benevolent organization, was established in New York City.

1899

A little more than 13,000 immigrants from Great Britain
arrived in the United States.

By 1899, the Chicago, Milwaukee and St. Paul Railroad retained only one immigration agent in all of Great Britain. This was a definite indication that, for all intents and purposes, emigration from the British Isles to the United States had just about stopped.

In 1899, British emigrants' declaration of resources to Ellis Island officials averaged about $70 per head.

By the end of the nineteenth century, most of the textile unions in New England were in the hands of English and Scottish labor leaders.

1900

After 1900, Englishmen and Scots, though leaving the homeland in unprecedented numbers, were now going to the Dominions rather than to the United States. In 1900, only 12,509 emigrants from Great Britain entered the country.

By 1900, a large number of Scotch-Irish immigrants and their descendents had achieved distinction as American statesmen. This list is long, and would include such men as Thomas Hart Benton, John C. Calhoun, Marcus Alonzo Hanna, and Horace Greeley.

After 1900, British potters practically ceased to emigrate to the United States.

Of all the ethnic groups arriving well before the end of the nineteenth century, the Welsh saw the decline of their language in church by 1900. First, one service in church in English each Sunday, then Welsh every other week, then Welsh once a month, until by the 1960's, only a handful of churches had anything more than a St. David's Day Service in the old tongue.

Love of the homeland was not peculiar to British immigrants. But, they clung most tenaciously to old loyalties. As late as 1900, adult male British immigrants who had not applied for their first papers included 13 percent of both the English and Scotch, and 7 percent of the Welsh.

By 1900, more than 194,000 emigrants from the British Isles were living in areas of the trans-Mississippi West.

More than 20,000 people from Great Britain had been helped by the Poor Law authorities to emigrate to the United States by 1900.

Cornish and Welsh immigrants comprised the majority of the mining force in Montana, Utah and Arizona.

By 1900, the British in Boston had moved into the South and West ends of the city, nearest the central business districts, and made up a large percentage of the salesmen and clerks in that section of town.

In New Bedford and Fall River, Massachusetts, the heads of the textile trade schools were all English experts, who had emigrated some years earlier. The most famous was James Northrop.

Annual "Welsh Day" outings began to take place. The highlights of these celebrations were singing competitions and concerts. They attracted thousands of visitors at such centers as Scranton, Wilkes-Barre, and Pittsburgh.

1901

Cornish clubs in Chicago, Boston and New York began holding picnics, where games of the Old Country were played, and where participants ate traditional foods.

When Queen Victoria died, British-Americans across the country, thronged into the churches for a special memorial service. Other special occasions were marked by the British-American; coronations, births, and marriages.

When the United Textile Workers of America, the first important national union in the trade, was formed, its mainstays were English and Scottish operatives from Fall River and New Bedford, Massachusetts.

1902

Emigration from the British Isles picked up a little, when more than 16,000 persons arrived in the United States.

The New York Police Department asserted that in most cases of robbery by servants in the city, English immigrants headed the list of culprits.

In 1902, the immigrant British weaver in America was earning about $11 a week.

Benjamin Talbot, an English immigrant, developed the Roe Puddler for use in the steel industry.

In 1903, American prosperity and British depression
released a new flood of immigrants, whose total reached the
highest level of emigration to the United States from Great
Britain in twenty years. More than 33,600 persons arrived in America.

Beginning in 1903, and lasting until 1914, more Britons
annually sailed from the United Kingdom than during any
previous dozen years. However, only one third of this
total emigration came to the United States, the majority
emigrating to the various dominions.

In 1903, the seven Illinois mine inspectorships were divided
among five Englishmen, a Scot, and a Welshman, while
the head of the state mining board was a Lancashire collier,
who had become a leading coal operator in the Peoria district.

The leading British residents of Boston, entertained the
visiting Grenadier Guards, and the Honourable Artillery
Company of London.

1904

British emigration to the United States continued to make
a comeback. In 1904, almost 52,000 Britons came to
America.

By 1904, British Presbyterian churches in New England
numbered nearly fifty, with more than 10,000 members.

Steerage fare to America dropped to $15, and as a result,
thousands of British workers emigrated to the United
States in this and the following year.

1905

By 1905, in most American industries where the British
workman had been dominant, these skilled hands lost
their places to peasant "greenhorns" of the "New Immigration."

The majority of workmen at the San Francisco shipyards
were Scottish immigrants.

This year was another peak period for British immigration
to the United States, as emigration from the British Isles
continued to surge upward. More than 84,000 Britons entered America.

1906

A British Parliamentary report concluded that Britons assimilated quickly and easily. And, indeed, few Americans used any nicknames to identify immigrants from Great Britain; they seldom thought of them, whether Scotch, English, or Welsh neighbors as foreigners.

The British continued to come to the United States, but in diminished numbers. Only 67,000 of them emigrated to America in 1906.

About 25 percent of the workers in the upholstery and drapery fabrics industry were English and Scotch.

The Welsh were a decreasing minority of the tinplate workers in the Pennsylvania mills.

The six Celtic races, the Scotch, Welsh, Cornish, Manx, Breton and Irish, merged their separate traditions in a unique Celtic Club in Boston.

On the invitation of the state of Virginia, several hundred British settlers emigrated to the Piedmont region.

By 1906, Scotch communities of granite quarrymen had been established at Quincy and Ware in Massachusetts, Vinalhaven and Rockland in Maine, and at Concord, New Hampshire.

1907

In 1907, 79,000 immigrants from Great Britain arrived in the United States.

By 1907, the gradual decline of the Welsh language put an end to all the Welsh newspapers and periodicals in the United States except Y Cyfaill and Y Drych.

An English language weekly, the Druid of Scranton and Pittsburgh began to be published, and claimed more than 12,000 subscribers.

As late as 1907, New Jersey carpet factories were predominantly staffed by Scots from Kidderminster.

In 1907, 56 percent of all woolen millworkers in the United States were of English origins, while 45 percent were of Scottish backgrounds.

A severe economic slump in Wales, sent slateworkers from Blaenau, Ffestiniog, Bethesda, and Nantile to the United States.

1908

Enough members of the British Carpenter's Union arrived in San Francisco to support eight American locals.

Beginning in 1908, such English societies as the Victorian Club of Boston, the British Empire Association of Chicago, and the British Empire Club of Providence, held banquets on Empire Day or on the anniversary of the Battle of Trafalgar.

1909

British emigration to the United States dropped to a little more than 46,000 persons.

British craftsmen from England and Scotland were brought to Grand Rapids, Michigan, to make fine morocco upholstered furniture.

The first British-American women's federation, wholly independent of any male society, The Imperial Order, Daughters of the British Empire, took root in New York City.

A Special Report of the United States Bureau of the Census entitled, A Century of Population Growth, indicated that in 1790, the English nationality, as revealed by the names of heads of families, formed 83.5 percent of the colonial white population.

1910

America's economic health being poorer than Britain's migration from the United Kingdom again declined.

British immigrants constituted seven percent of all those engaged in the glovemaking industry in America, the largest group living in Gloversville, New York.

By 1910, very few British silkworkers were emigrating to the United States.

At the United States Steel's Homestead plant, British immigrants formed 20 percent of the skilled workers, 12 percent of the semi-skilled, and only 2 percent of the unskilled workers, who were now made up of the "New Immigrants."

Dislike for the "New Immigrants" discouraged British colliers from entering American mining establishments, which, by 1910, seemed "a Hunkey's job" to them.

British immigrants made the highest daily wages of all immigrant groups in the United States.

The Welsh population in many of the old Pennsylvania mining towns had become almost nil.

1911

As late as 1911, the opening of new steel mills was still welcome news in Welsh-American communities, and new Welsh colonies sprang up in western iron centers such as Pueblo, Colorado.

The Dillingham Commission on Immigration reported that Scottish immigrants had the highest percentage of skilled laborers than any other immigrant group that had come to the United States.

There were 200 Welshmen working at the coal camp of Casbonado, Washington, while hundreds of British miners were still going into the coal fields of Kansas, Wyoming, Colorado, Utah and California.

The British continued to emigrate to the United States, some 73,000 of them arriving in 1911.

1912

All of the British societies of Boston observed the Dickens Centenary with banquets, lectures and parties.

1913

Although Slavic and Mediterranean immigrants replaced the British in the mines of America, most of the managers and superintendents were either Welsh or Scotch.

The choir of the largest Presbyterian church in Racine, Wisconsin was solidly Welsh.

September   The Gorsedd of the bards of Wales, sanctioned an American Gorsedd, and the Archdruid Dyfed, himself, crossed the Atlantic to preside over the Pittsburgh International Eisteddfod.

1914

By 1914, the Order of the Scottish Clans claimed 16,000 members located in 160 active local units.

Only five percent of the underground workers in the Pennsylvania coal fields were British-born. Most of the British had either left the mines, or had been replaced by new immigrant workers.

August 4   The entrance of Great Britain into World War I saw most Americans of British birth or descent become avidly pro-ally.

The outbreak of World War I caused a serious decline in British immigration to the United States. During 1914, only a little more than 48,000 people from the British Isles emigrated to America, and in the following years the number would drop still further.

1915

Total British emigration to the United States fell to only about 27,000.

By 1915, of all the British employed in the iron and steel industry, 47 percent were skilled workers, and 37 percent were semiskilled.

Statistics show that Englishmen and Scots owned and managed a greater share of the entire American textile industry than all other foreign groups put together.

June   Women in Ohio originated the National Women's Welsh-American Clubs, of which there were at least a dozen within the next three years.

October   The English Folk Dance Society of America was organized by Cecil Sharpe. It aimed to perpetuate and encourage folk dancing in its original and traditional for   he United States.

1917

British emigration to the United States continued to decline, with only 10,700 persons coming to America from
the British Isles.

In Boston, a kilted battalion of Scots, the McClean Highlanders was raised for the Canadian Overseas Forces.

John Spargo, a Cornish Socialist, who had been one of the
leaders of the American-Socialist party, broke with the
party because of its pacifist and pro-German policies.

April 6

When the United States entered World War I, British-
Americans rallied to the cause. Although no special Bri-
tish-American units were formed, thousands of men of
British birth or descent volunteered for military service.

1918

In 1918, British emigration to the United States reached
its lowest point in almost 200 years, when 2,600 Britons
entered the country.

By 1918, more than 40 percent of all the British working
people who had arrived in the United States, were engaged
in skilled trades industries.

In 1918, the Scottish Caledonian Clubs held a series of
games in more than 125 towns and cities across the United
States.

The London born Chicago utilities magnate, Samuel Insull,
raised millions of dollars for war relief and aid to Great
Britain.

Statistics indicated that few British professional men had
sailed as immigrants for America during the preceding
forty years.

November 11

The end of World War I, brought both relief and joy to
British-Americans. Their churches were filled as con-
gregants gave thanks for the victory.

1919

British emigration did not substantially rise, even though
the war had been concluded. Only a little more than
6,000 persons from the British Isles came to the United
States.

The Welsh Calvinistic Methodists voted to merge their general assembly with the Northern Presbyterians.

1920

A considerable increase in British immigration occurred, when 38,400 Britons came to America.

The Census of 1920, reported that of male British immigrants, 15 percent of the English and Scotch, and 9 percent of the Welsh had not begun the naturalization process to become American citizens.

In 1920, no immigrant nationality had a higher proportion of fully naturalized citizens than did the Welsh.   Still, they were attached to Wales, and to the "Queen of England."

British lace-makers filled the best jobs in the American lace industry as late as 1920.

The American upholstery and drapery fabrics industry continued to rely on British weavers.

1922

Despite the passage of the Immigration Law of 1921, which gave Great Britain a large quota of emigrants to the United States, barely 25,000 Britons entered the country. In fact, from 1922 to 1929, emigration totals from Great Britain to the United States remained fairly constant, never rising above 31,000, and never dropping below 19,000 in any one year, with the exception of 1924.

The first Odd Fellows in the United States were Englishmen. As early as 1843, they broke with the parent organization in London, and by 1922, the British-American Odd Fellows claimed 22,168 men, in 167 lodges, and 4,390 women in 61 lodges in cities and towns across the nation.

1924

The Immigration Act of 1924 raised the British emigrant quota, and Great Britain responded by sending 59,490 persons to the United States.   It was the largest group to come to America since 1913.

1925

Although English immigrants showed little of the Welsh or Scotch concern for Old Country culture, they nevertheless formed their own clubs and societies, and held their own festivals. By 1925, seventeen English clubs belonged to a New England Federation.

By 1925, the Welsh press in the United States had vanished. Not a single newspaper in the Welsh language was being published anymore.

1926

Beginning in 1926, the English Folk Dance Society of America conducted a summer school and Folk Dance Camp at Pinewoods Camp near Plymouth, Massachusetts.

1930

The 1930 Census listed 354,423 foreign-born Scotchmen living in the United States.

There were 60,205 foreign-born Welsh in the United States. Pennsylvania had the largest number of them, with New York, Ohio, Illinois and Michigan following next in order.

By 1930, 72.9 percent of all Welshmen in America had been naturalized, while only 60.9 of all foreign-born Scotsmen had become American citizens.

In 1930, there were 146,772 individuals who had been born in England residing in New York City. More than 67,000 persons of Scottish birth lived in New York, with lesser numbers in Pennsylvania, Michigan, Massachusetts, Illinois and California.

The St. Andrew's Society of Charleston, South Carolina, celebrated its 200th anniversary.

Immigrants from the United Kingdom made Old Country festival days the great patriotic occasion of the year in the United States. The English had their St. George's Day (April 23), the Scotch, their St. Andrew's Day (November 30), and the Welsh, their St. David's Day (March 1.) As late as 1930, these holidays were still being celebrated although in diminished form.

1931

From 1931 to 1940, British immigration to the United
States never exceeded 9,000 in any one year.

1933

British immigration to the United States hit an all time low,
when only 979 persons arrived in the country.

1935

No newspapers designed solely for English immigrants
lasted very long, although there were a number of them
published. throughout the nineteenth and into the twentieth
centuries. By 1935, not one single English-American
newspaper or journal was still in existence.

1936

By 1936, several organizations had been formed to promote
Anglo-American relations. They included, The General
Society of Mayflower Descendents, The Ark and Dove, The
Colonial Dames of America, and The Hereditary Descend-
ents of Colonial Governors.

1937

Coincidental with the 350th anniversary of the founding of
Roanoke Island colony, was the discovery of a quartz stone
at Chowan County, North Carolina, carved with what was
purported to be a message from Eleanore White Dare,
Virginia Dare's mother, describing the slaughter of the
entire colony by Indians. This "find" was followed by
48 others, all seeming to corroborate the first, but they
were all exposed as forgeries by Boyden Sparkes in 1941.

1939

By 1939, Y Drych was the only surviving Welsh-American
newspaper, but for several years, it had been printed in
English.

September 1   The outbreak of World War II in Europe found British-
Americans, once again, solidly pro-ally. During the late
1930's, they had supported President Franklin D. Roose-
velt's attempts to modify the nation's policy of neutrality,
and they now clamored for more American aid to their
homeland.

1940

The Census of 1940, showed that up to that date, a total of 4,321,590 people from Great Britain had come to the United States. They included 2,700,000 English, 87,000 Welsh, and 1,534,590 Scotch and Scotch-Irish.

In 1940, New York City contained the largest totals of British immigrants than any other single place in the United States. There were 178,000 English, 71,000 Scots, 79,000 Scotch-Irish, and 5,000 Welsh in its total population.

The annual Welsh Eisteddfod at Jackson, Ohio, began attracting national attention, although the Eisteddfod at Utica, New York, usually held on New Year's Day, was the best known of the Welsh musical and literary competitions. Church singing and community singing were the greatest recreation of the Welsh in the United States.

As a result of the outbreak of World War II in Europe, British immigration to the United States virtually stopped, never again to recover its normal flow, except during the years immediately following the conclusion of the war, when war brides and displaced persons were allowed to enter the country in relatively large numbers.

EPILOGUE to BRITISH IMMIGRATION--1940-1970

By 1910, when the British-American community had finally emerged, its English, Scottish, and Welsh components had already begun to shrink in size. Emigrants leaving the United Kingdom were no longer coming to the United States. The First World War considerably cut into British immigration, and, in fact, when the conflagration had terminated, the British movement to America was done. A brief revival occurred in 1923-1924, but by this time, the United States had little to offer the British. Moreover, the United States was putting up bars against foreigners, and although the quota acts of 1921 and 1924 permitted Great Britain a relatively high annual quota, the British seldom filled a quarter of their quota. The red tape of the late 1920's and the depression of the 1930's almost completely stopped their influx. When World War II began in 1939, British immigration declined still further, and during the war years of 1942 and 1943, it reached an all time low of 907 and 974 respectively. Between 1946 and 1949, a postwar rush of immigration accounted for a substantial increase, but even during the peak year of 1948, only 26,403 newcomers from the United Kingdom arrived in the United States. In the decade from 1950 to 1960, a total of approximately 170,000 immigrants from Great Britain came to America; in 1965, only 27,358, and in 1970, the total had dropped to 14,158. Therefore, the British, as a substantial immigrant group, have all but been eliminated by the decade of the 1970's.

Thus, the period from 1940 to 1970 saw the British-American community, reinforced from neither within or without, dwindle to a point where Americans of British origins were virtually indistinguishable. The Scottish and English newspapers passed into oblivion, and only the Welsh Y Drych continued to be published, although it had been reduced to a monthly, printed almost wholly in English. To be sure, many of the societies which existed at the turn of the century have continued to our present time or have been replaced by similar ones. New lodges of the Sons of St. George, the Order of Scottish Clans, the Loyal Orange Institution, the Daughters of the British Empire and others have been established during the past thirty years. But, they are few and far between, and the period of innovation has been terminated. Most of the British immigrant institutions are in a general decline as compared with their pre-1914 vigor. Moreover, it is almost impossible today to recognize Americans of British origins without delving deeply into their individual history and background. The economic and social adjustments of these peoples are and have been relatively so easy that they can and have entered into American affairs as equals of the natives of this country. In addition, we may say, that, in a sense, British-Americans have had no "second generation," no ill adjusted class, like the children of less fortunate foreigners. In effect, the children of British immigrants were simply Americans, neither better nor worse adapted to the normal life of the United States than were the children of native parents. They seldom thought of themselves as British, and always looked at themselves, and each other, as Americans.

Finally then, the period from 1940 to 1970 has been one in which no appreciable numbers of immigrants from the United Kingdom have come to America, and one in which no unique or distinguishable contributions to American life and society have been made by this enigmatic British-American community. Rather, the period from 1940 to 1970 has been a sort of epilogue to the very vigorous history of British immigration prior to the outbreak of World War I.

DOCUMENTS

The series of documents that follow have been culled from a variety of sources. Although they represent only a small fragment of primary materials concerned with British immigration, they will, nevertheless provide the reader with a good overall picture of the mass movement of those peoples who came to America from the British Isles. Because of the very nature of British immigration to and in America, a large portion of the documentary materials concerns itself with the colonial period of American history. Selectivity has been a major problem, for, in essence, the early history of British immigration, is, basically, the early history of America, and it would have been impossible to include documents covering every aspect of British life in Colonial America. As a result, the documents were chosen to present as varied a picture of the British experience in this country as possible. As one might expect, the documents concerned with British immigration are not housed in any one repository, but are scattered throughout the country in many different places. Despite this difficulty, the interested student, once having begun research into this topic, will shortly become aware of the location and value of the materials he is seeking. It is the purpose of this section of this book to provide a good starting point for such research.

Typical of the enthusiasm with which Englishmen of the late sixteenth century reported upon the new frontier in America, were
the reactions of two sea captains, who in 1584 were sent out by
Sir Walter Raleigh in connection with his efforts to exploit the
opportunities of the New World.
(Source: Robert Beverley, History and Present State of Virginia,
London, 1705.)

The Learned and Valiant Sir Walter Raleigh.... having laid together
the many Stories then in Europe concerning America; the Native Beauty,
Riches, and Value of this Part of the World; and the immense Profits the
Spaniards drew from a small Settlement or two thereon made; resolv'd upon
an Adventure for further Discoveries.

According to this Purpose, in the Year of our Lord, 1583, He got several Men of great Value and Estate to join with him in an Expedition of this
Nature: And for their Incouragement obtain'd Letters Patents from Queen
Elizabeth, bearing the date the 25th of March, 1584, for turning their Discoveries to their own Advantage ....

In April following they set out Two small Vessels under the Command
of Capt. Philip Amidas, and Capt. Arthur Barlow; who, after a prosperous
Voyage, anchor'd at the Inlet by Roenoke.... They made good Profit of the
Indian Truck, which they bought for Things of much inferior Value and return'd. Being over-pleased with their Profits, and finding all Things there
entirely new, and surprizing; they gave a very advantageous Account of
Matters; by representing the Country so delightful, and desirable; so pleasant, and plentiful the Climate, and Air, so temperate, sweet, and wholesome
the Woods, and Soil, so charming, and fruitful; and all other Things so
agreeable, that Paradice it self seem'd to be there in its first Native Lustre.

They gave particular Accounts of the Variety of good Fruits, and some
whereof they had never seen the Like before; but above all, that there were
Grapes in such abundance, as was never known in the World: Stately tall
large Oaks, and other Timber; Red Cedar, Cypress, Pines, and other Ever-
greens, and Sweetwoods; for tallness and largeness exceeding all they had
ever heard of: Wild Fowl, Fish, Deer, and other Game in such Plenty,
and Variety; that no Epicure could desire more than this New World did
seem naturally to afford.

And, to make it yet more desirable, they reported the Native Indians
(which were then the only Inhabitants) so affable, kind, and good-natur'd;
so uncultivated in Learning, Trades, and Fashions: so innocent, and ignorant of all manner of Politicks, Tricks, and Cunning; and so desirous of
the Company of the English: That they seem'd rather to be like soft Wax,
ready to take any Impression, than any ways likely to oppose the Settling of
the English near them ....

Her Majesty ... being so well pleased with the Account given, that as
the greatest Mark of Honour she could do the Discovery, she call'd the
Country by the Name of Virginia; ....

Various types of writings have always acted as a source of Propaganda motivating the British to emigrate to America. This selection, a scene from a seventeenth century play, is an early example of this type of promotional activity.
(Source: George Chapman, Ben Jonson, and John Marston, Eastward Hoe, London, 1605.) Reprinted in Alexander Brown, The Genesis of the United States . . . . A Series of Historical Manuscripts Now First Printed, I, Cambridge, Massachusetts, 1890.)

Act III., Scene 2.
Enter Seagull, Spendall, and Scapethrift in
the Blewe Anchor Taverne, with a Drawer.

. . . Seagull. Come, boyes, Virginia longs till we share the rest of her maiden-head.
Spendall. Why, is she inhabited alreadie with an English?
Seagull. A whole countrie of English is there, man, bread of those that were left there in '79; they have married with the Indians, and make 'hem bring forth as beautifull faces as any we have in England; and therefore the Indians are so in love with 'hem, that all the treasures they have they lay at their feete.
Scapethrift. But is there such treasure there, Captaine, as I have heard?
Seagull. I tell thee, golde is more plentifull there than copper is with us; and for as much redde copper as I can bring Ile have thrise the waight in gold. Why, man, all their dripping-pans and their chamber-potts are pure gould; and all the chaines with which they chaine up their streets are massie gold; all the prisoners they take are fetered in gold; and for rubies and diamonds they goe forth on holydayes and gather 'hem by the sea-shore to hang on their childrens coates and sticke in their children's caps, as commonly as our children weare saffron-gilt brooches and groates with hoales in 'hem.
Scapethrift. And is it a pleasant countrie withall?
Seagull. As ever the sunne shin'd on: temperate and ful of all sorts of excellent viands; wilde bore is as common there as our tamest bacon is here; venison as mutton. And then you shall live freely there, without sargeants, or courtiers, or lawyers, or intelligencers . . . . Then for your meanes to advancement, there it is simple, and not preposterously mixt. You may bee an alderman here, and never be a scavinger; you may be any other officer, and never be a pandar; to riches, and fortunes enough and have never the more villanie nor the lesse witte. Besides, there wee shall have no more law then conscience, and not too much of eyther; serve God enough, eate and drinke inough, and "enough is as good as a feast."
Spendall. Gods me! and how farre is it thether?
Seagull. Some six weekes saile, no more, with any indifferent good winde.

The following selection is a petition to Parliament by an unknown author, who explains, in detailed form, the public interest in New World colonization.
(Source: "Reasons to Move the High Court of Parliament to Raise a stock for Maintaining a Colony in Virginia," London, January 5, 1607; reprinted in Alexander Brown, Genesis of the United States, I, Cambridge, Massachusetts, 1890.)

Reasons or motives for the raising of a public stock to be employed for the peopling and discovering of such countries as may be found most convenient for the supply of those defects which this realm of England most requireth.

1. All kingdoms are maintained by rents or traffic, but especially by the latter, which in maritime places most flourishes by means of navigation.

2. The realm of England is an island impossible to be otherwise fortified than by strong ships and able mariners and is secluded from all corners . . . of the main continent; therefore fit abundance of vessels   must be prepared to export and import merchandise.

3. The furniture of shipping consists in masts, cordage, pitch, tar, rosin, that of which England is by nature unprovided and at this present enjoys them only by the favor of foreign potency.

4. The life of shipping rests in   the   number of able mariners and worthy chieftains, which cannot be maintained without assurance of reward of honorable means to be employed and sufficient second of their adventures.

5. Private purses are cold comforts to adventurers and have ever been found fatal to all enterprises hitherto undertaken by the English by reason of delays, jealousies and unwillingness to back that project which succeeded not at the first attempt.

6. The example of Hollanders is very pregnant . . . .

7. It is honorable for a state rather to back an exploit by a public consent than by a private monopoly.

8. Where colonies are founded for a public-weal,   they   may continue in better obedience, and become more industrious, than where private men are absolute . . . for as much as better men . . . will engage themselves in a public service, which carries more reputation with it, than a private, which is for the most part ignominious in the end, as being presumed to aim at a lucre . . . .

9. The manifest decay of shipping and mariners and of many borough and post towns and havens cannot be relieved by private increase . . . .

10. It is publicly known that traffic with our neighbor countries begin to be of small request, the game seldom answering the merchants' adventure . . . .

11. That realm is most complete and wealthy which either has sufficient to serve itself or can find the means to export of the natural commodities than   if   it has occasion necessarily to import.   Consequently it must ensue that by a public consent, a colony transported into a good and plentiful climate able to furnish our wants, our monies and wares that now

run into the hands of our adversaries or cold friends shall pass unto our friends and natural kinsmen and from them likewise we shall receive such things as shall be most available to our necessities, which intercourse of trade may rather be called a home bred traffic than a foreign exchange. . .

13. Experience teaches us that it is dangerous to our state to enterprise a discovery and not to proceed therein even to the very sifting it to the uttermost, for . . . disreputation grows thereby, . . . betraying our own idleness and want of counsel to manage our enterprises. . . .

14. The want of our fresh . . . discoveries has in manner taken away the title which the law of nations gives us into the coast first found out by our industry, forasmuch as whatsoever a man relinquishes may be claimed by the next finder as his own property. Neither is it sufficient to set foot in a country but to possess and hold it, in defense of an invading force.

For wnat whereof the King of Denmark intends into the northwest passage (as it is reported), and it is also reported that the French intend to inhabit Virginia . . . .

The circumstances necessary to back a colony sent out are these:

1. Reputation and opinion of the enterprise.

2. A competent sum of money raised aforehand to supply all accidents, that distrust hereby may be wrought in foreign states to attempt anything in prejudice of our colonies; because they may well be assured that where there is not a public purse, and a common consent to prosecute an action it is but hopeless to hope of advantage to be gotten without revenge.

3. As states are most apt to make a conquest so are public-weals fitter to hold what is gotten and skillfuller by industry to enrich it.

4. It is probable that if the whole state be engaged in these adventures it will be no hard matter when apparent ground of profit is laid to persuade every county according to the proportion of bigness and ability to build barks and ships of a component size and to maintain them, when gentlemen's youngest sons and other men of quality may be employed.

5. Also it importeth much that no man be suffered to venture more than he may be deemed able to spare out of his own superfluity, or if he go in person than he would idly spend at home, lest such men entering into a rage of repentance, . . . thereby discourage others and scandalize the enterprise.

> This selection is part of an account of the first permanent English settlement in America, Jamestown, Virginia, written by Captain John Smith, who can be credited with saving the colony from disaster.
> (Source: Lyon Gardiner Tyler, ed., Narratives of Early Virginia, New York, 1907.)

Virginia is a Country in America, that lyeth betweene the degrees of 34 and 44 of the north latitude. The bounds thereof on the East side are the great Ocean. On the South lyeth Florida: on the North nova Francia. As for the West thereof, the limits are unknowne. Of all this country wee purpose not to speake, but only of that part which was planted by the English men in the yeare of our Lord, 1606. And this is under the degrees, 37, 38, and 39. The temperature of this countrie doth agree well with English constitutions being once seasoned to the country. Which appeared by this, that though by many occasions our people fell sicke; yet did they recover by very small meanes and continued in health, though there were other great causes, not only to have made them sicke, but even to end their daies, etc.

The sommer is hot as in Spaine; the winter colde as in Fraunce or England. The heat of sommer is in June, Julie, and August, but commonly the coole Breeses asswage the vehemencie of the heat. The chiefe of winter is halfe December, January, February, and halfe March. The colde is extreame sharpe, but here the proverbe is true that no extreame long continueth.

In the yeare 1607, was an extraordinary frost in most of Europe, and this frost was founde as exteeame in Virginia. But the next yeare for 8 or 10 daies of ill weather, other 14 daies would be as Sommer.

The windes here are variable, but the like thunder and lightning to purifie the aire, I have seldome either seene or heard in Europe. From the Southwest came the greatest gustes with thunder and heat. The Northwest winde is commonly coole, and bringeth faire weather with it. From the Northe is the greatest cold, and from the East and South-East as from the Barmadas, fogs and raines.

Some times there are great droughts, other times much raine, yet great necessity of neither, by reason we see not but that all the variety of needfull fruits in Europe may be there in great plenty by the industry of men, as appeareth by those we there planted.

There is but one entraunce by sea into this country, and that is at the mouth of a very goodly Bay, the widenesse whereof is neare 18 or 20 miles. The cape on the South side is called Cape Henry in honour of our most noble Prince. The shew of the land there, is a white hilly sand like unto the Downes, and along the shores great plentie of Pines and Firres.

The north Cape is called Cape Charles in honour of the worthy Duke of Yorke. Within is a country that may have the prerogative over the most

pleasant places of Europe, Asia, Africa, or America, for large and pleasant navigable rivers: heaven and earth never agreed better to frame a
place for mans habitation being of our constitutions, were it fully manured
and inhabited by industrious people. Here are mountaines, hils, plaines,
valleyes, rivers and brookes all running most pleasantly into a faire Bay
compassed but for the mouth with fruitfull and delightsome land. In the
Bay and rivers are many Isles both great and small, some woody, some
plaine, most of them low and not inhabited. This Bay lieth North and South
in which the water floweth neare 200 miles and hath a channell for 140
miles, of depth betwixt 7 and 15 fadome, holding in breadth for the most
part 10 or 14 miles. From the head of the Bay at the north, the land is
mountanous, and so in a manner from thence by a Southwest line; So that the
more Southward, the farther off from the Bay are those mounetaines.
From which, fall certaine brookes, which after come to five principall navigable rivers. These run from the Northwest into the South east, and so
into the west side of the Bay, where the fall of every River is within 20 or
15 miles one of an other.

The mountaines are of diverse natures, for at the head of the Bay the
rockes are of a composition like miln-stones. Some of marble, &c. And
many peeces of christall we found as throwne downe by water from the
mountaines. For in winter these mountaines are covered with much snow,
and when it dissolveth the waters fall with such violence, that it causeth
great inundations in the narrow valleyes which yet is scarce perceived being
once in the rivers. These waters wash from the rocks such glistering tinc-
tures that the ground in some places seemeth as guilded, where both the
rocks and the earth are so splendent to behold, that better judgements then
ours might have beene perswaded, they contained more then probabilities.
The vesture of the earth in most places doeth manifestly prove the nature of
the soile to be lusty and very rich. The coulor of the earth we found in
diverse places, resembleth bole Armoniac, terra sigillata ad lemnia,
Fullers earth, marle, and divers other such appearances. But generally for
the most part the earth is a black sandy mould, in some places a fat slimy
clay, in other places a very barren gravell. But the best ground is knowne
by the vesture it beareth, as by the greatnesse of trees or abundance of
weedes, &c.   The country is not mountanous nor yet low but such pleasant plaine hils and fertle valleyes, one prettily crossing an other, and wa-
tered so conveniently with their sweete brookes and christall springs, as if
art itselfe had devised them. By the rivers are many plaine marishes
containing some 20, some 100, some 200 Acres, some more, some lesse.
Other plaines there are fewe, but only where the Savages inhabit: but all
overgrowne with trees and weedes being a plaine wildernes . . . .

Governor Thomas Gates of the Jamestown Colony was unable to
stop the trend toward social disorganization in the settlement,
and as a result he advocated the abandonment of Jamestown. In
this selection, he presented a harsh view of Virginia's first
settlers.
(Source: "A True Declaration of the Estate of the Colonie of
Virginian," in Albert B. Hart, ed., American History Told by
Contemporaries, I, New York, 1897.)

No man ought to judge of any Countrie by the fennes and marshes
(such as is the place where James towne standeth) except we will condemne
all England, for the Wilds and Hundreds of Kent and Essex. In our particular, wee have an infallible proofe of the temper of the Countrie . . . .

If any man shall accuse these reports of partiall falshood, supposing
them to be but Utopian, and legendarie fables, because he cannot conceive,
that plentie and famine, a tampareate climate, and distempered bodies,
felicities, and miseries can be reconciled together, let him now reade with
judgement, but let him not judge before he hath read . . . .

Now, I demand whether Sicilia, or Sardinia, (sometimes the barnes of
Rome) could hope for increase without manuring. A Colony is therefore
denominated, becuase they should be Coloni, the tillers of the earth, and
stewards of fertilitie: our mutinous loiterers would not sow with providence, and therefore they reaped the fruits of too deare bought repentance.
An incredible example of their idlenes, is the report of Sir Thomas Gates,
who affirmeth, that after his first coming thither, he had seen some of them
eat their fish raw, rather than they would go a stones cast to fetch wood
and dresse it, Di j laboribus omnia vendunt, God sels us all things for our
labour, when Adam himselfe might not live in paradice without dressing
the garden.

Unto idleness, you may joyne treasons, wrought by those unhallowed
creatures that forsooke the Colony, and exposed their desolate brethren to
extreame miserie. You shall know that 28 or 30 of the companie, were
appointed (in the Ship called the Swallow) to truck for Corne with the Indians, and having obtained a great quantitie by trading, the most seditious
of them conspired together, persuaded some, & enforced others to this
barbarous project. They stole away the Ship, they made a league amongst
themselves to be professed pirates, with dreames of mountaines of gold,
and happy roberies: thus at one instant, they wronged the hopes, and sub-
verted the cares of the Colony, who depended upon their returne, fore-
slowed to looke out for further provision: they created the Indians our
implacable enemies by some violence they had offered: they carried away
the best Ship (which should have been a refuge, in extremities) they weakened our forces, by substraction of their armes, and succours. These are
that scum of men that fayling in their piracy, that beeing pinched with
famine and penurie, after their wilde roving upon the Sea, when all their
lawlesse hopes failed, some remained with other pirates, they met upon the
Sea, the others resolved to returne to England, bound themselves by mutuall

oath, to agree all in one report, to discredit the land, to deplore the famyne, and to protest that this thier comming awaie, proceeded from desperate necessitie: . . .

Unto Treason, you may joyne covetousnesse in the Mariners, who for their private lucre partly imbezled the provisions, partly prevented our trade with the Indians, making the matches in the night, and forestalling our market in the day: whereby the Virginians were glutted with our trifles, and inhaunced the prices of their Corne and Victuall. That Copper which before would have provided a bushell, would not now obtaine so much as a pottle; Non habet eventus fordida preda bones, the consequent of sordid gaine is untimely wretchednesse.

Joyne unto these an other evill: there is great store of Fish in the river, especially of Sturgeon; but our men provided no more of them then for present necessitie, not barrelling up any store against that season the Sturgeon returned to the sea. And not to dissemble their folly, they suffered fourteene nets (which was all they had) to rot and spoile which by orderly drying and mending might have been preserved: but being lost, all help of fishing perished. Quanto maiora timentur dispendis tanto promptior debet esse cautela, fundamentall losses that cannot be repealed, ought with the greatest caution to be prevented.

The state of the Colony, by these accidents began to find a sensible declyning: which Powhatan (as a greedy Vulture) observing, and boyling with desire of revenge, he invited Captaine Ratclife, and about thirty others to trade for Corne, and under the colour of fairest friendship, he brought them within the compasse of his ambush, whereby they were cruelly murthered, and massacred . . . .

Cast up this reckoning together: want of government, store of idlenesse, their expectations frustrated by the Traitors, their market spoyled by the Mariners, our nets broken, the deere chased, our boats lost, our hogs killed, our trade with the Indians forbidden, some of our men fled, some murthered, and most by drinking of the brackish water of James fort weakened, and indaungered, famyne and sicknesse by all these meanes increase, here at home the monies came in so slowly, that the Lo. Laware could not be dispatched, till the Colony was worne and spent with dificulties: Above all, having neither Ruler, nor Preacher, they neither feared God nor man, which provoked the wrath of the Lord of Hosts, and pulled downe his judgements upon them, Discite Justitiam moniti, Now, (whether it were that God in mercie to us would weede out these ranke hemlockes; or whether in judgment to them he would scourge their impieties; or whether in wisedome he would trie our patience, Vt magna desiseremus, that wee may beg great blessins earnestly) our hope is that our Sunne shall not set in a cloude, since this violent storme is dispersed, Since all necessarie things are provided, an absolute and powerful government is setled, as by this insuing relation shall be described . . . .

It was not easy to get settlers for the Virginia Colony. This selection is part of an advertisement issued by the Council of Virginia for men of practical skills.
(Source: "A Publication of the Counsell of Virginia, touching the Plantation there," in Alexander Brown, The Genesis of the United States, I, Cambridge, Massachusetts, 1890.)

HOWSOEVER it came to passe by God's appointment, that governes all things, that the fleete of 8 shippes, lately sent to Virginea by meanes the Admiral, wherein were shipped the chiefe Governours, Sir Thomas Gates, Sir George Sommers and Captaine Newport, by the tempestuous windes and forcible current, were driven so farre to the Westward, that they could not in so convenient time recover Cape Henrie, and the Port in Virginea, as by the return of the same fleete to answer the expectation of the adventurers in some measure.

By occasion whereof, some few of those unruly youths sent thither, (being of most leaud and bad condition) and such as no ground can hold for want of good directions there, were suffered by stealth to get aboard the ships returning thence, and are come for England againe, giving out in all places where they come (to colour their own misbehaviour, and the cause of their returne with some pretence) most vile and scandalous reports, both of the Country itself, and of the Cariage of the businesse there.

Which hath also given occasion that sundry false rumours and despightfull speeches have been devised and given out by men that seeme of better sort, being such as lie at home, and doe gladly take all occasions to cheere themselves with the prevention of happy successe in any action of publike good, disgracing both the actions and actors of such honourable enterprises, as whereof they neither know nor understand the true intente and honest ends. . . . . .

And for that former experience hath too dearely taught, how much and manie waies it hurteth to suffer Parents to disburden themselves of lascivious sonnes, masters of bad servants and wives of ill husbands, and so to clogge the businesse with such an idle crue, as did thrust themselves in the last voiage, that will rather starve for hunger, than lay their hands to labor.

It is therefore resolved, that no such unnecessary person shall now be accepted, but onely such sufficient, honest and good artificers, as Smiths, Shipwrights, Sturgeon-dressers, Joyners, Carpenters, Gardeners, Turners, Coopers, Salt-makers, Iron-men for Furnasse & hammer, Brickmakers, Brick-layers, Minerall-men, Bakers, Gun-founders, Fishermen, Plough-wrights, Brewers, Sawyers, Fowlers, Vine-dressers, Surgeons and Physitions for the body, and learned Divines to instruct the Colonie, and to teach the Infidels to Worship the true God. Of which so many as will repair to the house of Sir Thomas Smith, Treasurer of the Company to proffer their service in this action, before the number be full, and will put in good sureties to be readie to attend the said honourable Lord in the voyage, . . .

82

In 1620, a hearty band of religious dissenters, known as the Pilgrims, decided to emigrate to the New World. In this selection, William Bradford, one of their leaders, expressed their hopes and fears.
(Source: William Bradford, Bradford's History of Plimoth Plantation, Boston, 1899.)

As necessitie was a taskmaster over them, so they were forced to be such, not only to their servants, but in a sorte, to their dearest children; the which as it did not a little wound ye tender harts of many a loving father & mother, so it produced likwise sundrie sad & sorowful effects. For many of their children, that were of best dispositions and gracious inclinations, haveing lernde to bear ye yoake in their youth, and willing to bear parte of their parents burden, were, often times, so oppressed with their hevie labours, that though their minds were free and willing, yet their bodies bowed under ye weight of ye same, and became decreped in their early youth; the vigor of nature being consumed in ye very budd as it were. But that which was more lamentable, and of all sorowes most heavie to be borne, was that many of their children, by these occasions, and ye great licentiousnes of youth in yt country . . . were drawne away by evill examples into extravagante & dangerous courses, getting ye raines off their neks, & departing from their parents.

These, & some other like reasons, moved them to undertake this resolution of their removall; the which they afterward prosecuted with so great difficulties . . . .

The place they had thoughts on was some of those vast & unpeopled countries of America, which are frutfull & fitt for habitation, being devoyd of all civill inhabitants, wher ther are only salvage & brutish men, which range up and downe, litle otherwise then ye wild beasts of the same. This proposition being made publike and coming to ye scaning of all, it raised many variable opinions amongst men, and caused many fears & doubts amongst themselves . . . .

It was answered, that all great & honourable actions are accompanied with great difficulties, and must be both enterprised and overcome with answerable courages. It was granted ye dangers were great, but not desperate; the difficulties were many, but not invincible . . . .

Having reached American shores, the Pilgrims, without a patent
to the land they wished to occupy, and without an official charter,
wrote their own Mayflower Compact, introduced in this selection
by William Bradford.
(Source: William Bradford, Bradford's History of Plimoth Plantation, Boston, 1899.)

A combination made by them before they came ashore, being the first
foundation of their govermente in this place; occasioned partly by the dis-
contented & mutinous speeches that some of the strangers amongst them had
let fall from them in the ship---That when they came a shore they would use
their owne libertie; for none had power to comand them, the patente they had
being for Virginia, and not for New-england, which belonged to an other Government, with which the Virginia Company had nothing to doe. And partly
that shuch an acte by them done (this their condition considered) might be
as firme as any patent, and in some respects more sure.
The forme was as followeth.

In the name of God, Amen. We whose names are underwriten, the
loyall subjects of our dread soveraigne Lord, King James, by the grace of
God, of Great Britaine, Franc, & Ireland king, defender of the faith, &c.,
haveing undertaken, for the glorie of God, and advancemente of the Christian
faith, and honour of our king & countrie, a voyage to plant the first colonie in
the Northerne parts of Virginia, doe by these presents solemnly & mutualy
in the presence of God, and one of another, covenant & combine our selves
togeather into a civill body politick, for our better ordering & preservation
& furtherance of the ends aforesaid; and by vertue hereof to enacte, constitute, and frame such just & equall lawes, ordinances, acts, constitutions, &
offices, from time to time, as shall be thought most meete & convenient for
the generall good of the Colonie, unto which we promise all due submission
and obedience. In witnes whereof we have hereunder subscribed our names
at Cap-Codd the 11 of November, in the year of the raigne of our soveraigne
lord, King James, of England, France, & Ireland the eighteenth, and of Scotland the fiftie fourth anno Domini 1620.

The first representative assembly in British North America was established in Virginia in 1619. The original document authorizing this assembly has been lost, but the company ordinance which follows is assumed similar to it.

(Source: Francis Newton Thorpe, comp. and ed., The Federal and State Constitutions, Colonial Charters, and Other Organic Laws of the States, Territories, and Colonies Now Forming the United States of America, VII, Washington, Government Printing Office, 1909.)

To all People, to whom these Presents shall come, be seen, or heard, The Treasurer, Council, and Company of Adventurers and Planters for the City of London for the first Colony of Virginia, send Greeting. Know ye, that we, the said Treasurer, Council, and Company, taking into our careful Consideration the presenth, state of the said Colony of Virginia, and intending, by the Divine Assistance, to settle such a Form of Government there, as may be to the greatest Benefit and Comfort of the People, and whereby all Injustice, Grievances, and Oppression may be prevented and kept off as much as possible from the said Colony, have thought fit to make our Entrance, by ordering and establishing such Supreme Councils, as may not only be assisting to the Governor for the time being, in the Administration of Justice, and the executing of other Duties to this office belonging, but also, by their vigilant care and Prudence, may provide, as well for a Remedy of all Inconveniences, growing from time to time, as also for advancing of Increase, Strength, Stability, and Prosperity of the said Colony:

II. We therefore, the said Treasurer, Council, and Company, by Authority directed to us from his Majesty under the Great Seal, uppon mature Deliberation, do hereby order and declare, that, from hence forward, there shall be TWO SUPREME COUNCILS in Virginia, for the better Government of the said Colony aforesaid.

III. The one of which Councils, to be called THE COUNCIL OF STATE (and whose Office shall chiefly be assisting, with their Care, Advise, and Circumspection, to the said Governor) shall be chosen, nominated, placed and displaced, from time to time by Us, the said Treasurer, Council, and Company, and our Successors . . . . Which said Counsellors and Council we earnestly pray and desire, and in his Majesty's Name strictly charge and command, that (all Factions, Partialities and sinister Respect laid aside) they bend their Care and Endeavours to assist the said Governor; first and principally, in the Advancement of the Honour and Service of God, and the Enlargement of his Kingdom amongst the Heathen People; and next, in erecting of the said Colony in due obedience to His Majesty; and all lawful Authority from his Majesty's Directions; and lastly, in maintaining the said People in Justice and Christian Conversation amongst themselves, and in strength and Ability to withstand their Enemies. And this Council, to be always, or for the most Part, residing about or near the Governor.

IV.   The other Council, more generally to be called by the Governor, once yearly, and no oftener, but for very extraordinary and important occasions, shall consist, for the present, of the said Council of State, and of two Burgesses out of every Town, Hundred, or other particular Plantation, to be respectively chosen by the Inhabitants: Which Council shall be called THE GENERAL ASSEMBLY, wherein (as also in the said Council of State) all Matters shall be decided, determined, and ordered, by the greater Part of the Voices then present; reserving to the Governor always a Negative Voice.   And this General Assembly shall have free Power to treat, consult, and conclude, as well of all emergent Occasions concerning the Publick Weal of the said Colony and every Part thereof, as also to make, ordain, and enact such general Laws and Orders, for the Behoof of the said Colony, and the good Government thereof, as shall, from time to time, appear necessary or requisite;

V.   Whereas in all other Things, we require the said General Assembly, as also the said Council of State, to imitate and follow the policy of the Form of Government, Laws, Customs, and Manner of Trial, and other Administration of Justice, used in the Realm of England, as near as may be, even as ourselves, by his Majesty's Letters Patent, are required.

VI.   Provided, that no Law or Ordinance, made in the said General Assembly, shall be or continue in Force or Validity, unless the same shall be solemnly ratified and confirmed, in a General Quarter Court of the said Company here in England and so ratified; be returned to them under our Seal; it being our Intent to afford the like Measure also unto the said Colony, that after the Government of the said Colony shall once have been well framed, and settled accordingly, which is to be done by Us, as by Authority derived from his Majesty, and the same shall have been so by us declared, no Orders of Court afterwards shall bind the said Colony, unless they be ratified in like Manner in the General Assemblies.

In 1629, a group of English Puritans received a charter from King Charles I for a grant of land in America. What follows is the charter that the Massachusetts Bay Company brought with them to America.
(Source: Founding of Massachusetts. A Selection From the Sources of the History of the Settlement, Boston, 1930.)

Charles, by the grace of God King of England, Scotland, France and Ireland, Defender of the Faith, etc. To all to whom these presents shall come. Greeting.

Whereas our most dear and royal father King James . . . hath . . . granted unto the council established at Plymouth . . . all that part of America lying . . . from forty degrees of northerly latitude . . . to forty-eight degrees of the said northerly latitude inclusively, and . . . from sea to sea . . . .

And whereas the said council established at Plymouth . . . have . . . given . . . to Sir Henry Rosewell . . . and others all that part of New England . . . which lies . . . between a great river there commonly called . . Merrimack, and a certain other river there called Charles River being in the bottom of a certain other river there called Charles River being in the bottom of a certain bay there commonly called Massachusetts . . . Bay. And also, all . . . lands . . . lying within . . . three English miles on the south part of the said Charles River . . . and also, all . . . lands . . . lying . . . within . . . three English miles to the southward of . . . Massachusetts Bay. And also all . . . lands . . . which lie . . . within . . . three English miles to the northward of the said river called Merrimack . . . from the Atlantic . . . Sea on the east, to the South Sea on the west . . . . And also all mines and minerals . . ., and all jurisdictions, rights, royalties, liberties, freedoms, immunities, privileges, franchises, preeminences and commodities whatsoever which . . . the . . . council established at Plymouth then had . . . . To be holden of us . . . as of our manor of East Greenwich in the county of Kent, in free and common socage, and not in capite, nor by knights' service. Yielding and paying therefore unto us . . . the fifth part of the ore of gold and silver which shall . . . be found, . . . in any of the said lands . . . in satisfaction of all manner duties . . . to be done . . . to us . . .

Now know ye that we, at the humble suit and petition of the said Sir Henry Rosewell, . . . and of others, . . . by this present . . . do grant and confirm . . . all the said part of New England . . . to them . . .

And forasmuch as the good and prosperous success of the plantation of the said parts of New England aforesaid . . . , cannot but chiefly depend, next under the blessing of almighty God, and the support of our royal authority upon the good government of the same, to the end that the affairs . . . concerning the said lands and the plantation . . . may be the better managed and ordered, we have further hereby . . . granted and confirmed . . . unto our said trusty and well beloved subjects named that they

. . . and all such others as shall hereafter be . . . made free of the company
. . . , shall . . . be . . . one body corporate and politic . . . by the name of
the Governor and Company of the Massachusetts Bay in New England . . .
And . . . by that name they shall have perpetual succession, and . . . shall
. . . be . . . enabled . . . to implead and to be impleaded . . . in all . . .
suits . . . and actions.

. . . And also to have, take, possess, acquire and purchase any lands,
tenements or hereditaments or any goods or chattels, and the same to lease,
grant, demise, alien, bargain, sell and dispose of, as other our liege people
of this our realm of England, or any other corporation or body politic of
the same may lawfully do. And further that the said governor and company
and their successors may have forever one common seal to be used in all
causes and occasions . . . .

And our will and pleasure is . . . that from henceforth forever there
shall be one governor, one deputy governor and eighteen assistants of the
same company to be from time to time. . . chosen out of the freemen of the
said company . . .; which said officers shall apply themselves to take care
for the best disposing and ordering of the general business . . . of . . . the
said lands and premises . . . and the government of the people there . . . .
   First officers named   . . . .

And further, we . . . do ordain . . . that the governor . . . or in his
absence . . . the deputy governor . . . shall have authority . . . to give order for the assembling of the said company, and calling them together to
consult and advise of the businesses . . . of the said company, and that the
said governor, deputy governor and assistants . . . shall or may once every
month or oftener . . . assemble, and hold . . . a court or assembly . . .
for the better ordering and directing of their affairs, and that any seven or
more persons of the assistants together with the governor or deputy governor so assembled shall be . . . a full and sufficient court or assembly of
the said company . . . And that there shall. . . be held . . . by the governor
or deputy governor of the said company and seven or more of the said assistants . . . upon every last Wednesday in Hillary, Easter, Trinity and Michas
Terms respectively forever, one great general and solemn assembly; which
four general assemblies shall be styled and called the four great and general
courts of the said company. In all and every, or any of which said great
and general courts so assembled . . . the governor, or in his absence the
deputy governor . . . and such of the assistants and freemen . . . as shall
be present, or the greater number of them . . . shall have full power . . .
to choose, . . . such . . . others as they shall think fit . . . to be free of the
said company; . . . and to elect and constitute such officers as they shall
think fit and requisite; . . . and to make laws and ordinances . . . for the
government and ordering of the said lands and plantation, and the people
inhabiting . . . the same, as to them from time to time shall be thought
meet. So as such laws and ordinances be not contrary or repugnant to
the laws and statutes of this our realm of England. And our will and
pleasure is . . . that . . . the last Wednesday in Easter Term yearly, the
governor, deputy governor and assistants of the said company, and all other
officers . . . shall be in the general court or assembly . . . newly chosen
for the year ensuing. . . . And if . . . the . . . governor, deputy governor and

assistants . . . or any other of the officers to be appointed for the said company . . . die, or . . . be removed from his or their several offices . . . before the said general day of election . . ., then . . . it shall . . . be lawful . . . for the governor, deputy governor, assistants and company aforesaid . . . in any of their assemblies to proceed to a new election . . . . Provided . . . that . . . all . . . officers to be appointed . . . shall before they undertake the execution of their said offices . . . take their corporal oaths for the . . . faithful performance of their duties in their several offices . . . .

And we do further . . . give and grant to the said governor and company . . . that it shall be lawful . . . for them . . . out of any our . . . dominions whatsoever, to take . . . into their voyages, and for and towards the said plantation in New England . . . so many of our loving subjects or any other strangers that will become our loving subjects . . . as shall willingly accompany them . . . and also shipping, armor, weapons, ordinance, munition, powder, shot, corn, victuals, and all manner of clothing, implements, furniture, beasts, cattle, horses, mares, merchandises, and all other things necessary for the said plantation . . . without paying . . . any custom or subsidy either inward or outward to us . . . for the same, by the space of seven years from the . . . date of these presents . . . And for their further encouragement, . . . we do . . . yield and grant to the said governor and company . . . that they . . . shall be free and quit from all taxes, subsidies and customs in New England for the like space of seven years, and from all taxes and impositions for the space of twenty and one years upon all goods and merchandises at any time or times hereafter, either upon importation thither, or exportation from thence into our realm of England, or into any other   of   our dominions . . . except only the five pounds per centum due for custom . . . after the said seven years shall be thenceforth lawful and free for the said adventurers the same goods and merchandises to export and carry out of our said dominions into foreign parts, without any custom, tax or other duty . . . .

Mode of paying customs   . . . .

And further . . . we do hereby . . . grant to the said governor and company . . . that all . . . the subjects of us, our heirs or successors which shall go to . . . the said lands . . . and . . . their children . . . born there, or on the seas in going thither, or returning from thence shall . . . enjoy all liberties and immunities of free and natural subjects within any of the dominions of us, our heirs or successors to all intents, constructions and purposes whatsoever, as if they . . . were born within the realm of England. And that the governor and deputy governor of the said company . . . and any two or more of such of the said assistants, as shall be thereunto appointed by the said governor and company at any of their courts or assemblies . . . may at all times . . . have full power and authority to minister and give the . . . oaths of supremacy and allegiance . . . to all . . . persons which shall at any time . . . hereafter go . . . to the lands . . . hereby mentioned to be granted . . . .

And we do . . . grant to the said governor and company . . . that it shall . . . be lawful . . . for the governor or deputy governor and such of the assistants and freemen of the said company . . . as shall be assembled

in any of their general courts ... or the greater part of them . . . from time
to time to make . . . all manner of wholesome and reasonable orders, laws,
statutes and ordinances . . . not contrary to the laws of this our realm of
England, as well for settling of the forms and ceremonies of government and
magistracy fit and necessary for the said plantation and the inhabitants
there, and for naming and styling all sorts of officers . . . which they shall
find needful . . . , and the distinguishing, and setting forth of the several
duties, powers and limits of every such office and place and the forms of
such oaths . . . as shall be respectively ministered unto them for the execution of the said several offices and places, as also for the disposing and
ordering of the elections of such of the said officers as shall be annual,
. . . and ministering the said oaths to the new elected officers and for impositions of lawful fines, mulcts, imprisonment or other lawful correction,
according to the course of other corporations in this our realm of England.
And for the directing, ruling and disposing of all other matters and things
whereby our said people inhabitants there may be so religiously, peaceably
and civilly governed, as their good life and orderly conversation may win
and incite the natives of   the   country to the knowledge and obedience of
the only true God and Saviour of mankind, and the Christian faith, which is
. . . the principal end of this plantation. Willing, commanding and requir-
ing . . . that all such orders, laws, statutes and ordinances . . . as shall be
so made . . . and published in writing . . . , shall be carefully and duly observed . . . and put in execution according to the true intent and meaning
of the same. And these our letters patents . . . shall be . . . for the putting
of the same orders, laws, statutes, and ordinances . . . a sufficient warrant
and discharge.

And we do further . . . grant to the said governor and company . . .
that all . . . such . . . officers and ministers, as . . . shall be . . . employed
either in the government of the said inhabitants and plantation, or in the
way by sea thither, or from thence . . . shall . . . have full and absolute
power and authority to correct, punish, pardon, govern and rule all such
. . . subjects . . . as shall from time to time adventure themselves in any
voyage thither or from thence, or that shall at any time hereafter inhabit
. . . New England . . ., according to the orders, laws, ordinances, instructions and directions aforesaid, not being repugnant to the laws and statutes of our realm of England . . . .

And we do further . . . grant to the said governor and company . . .
that it shall . . . be lawful . . . for the chief commanders, governors and
officers of the said company . . . for their special defense and safety to
encounter, expulse, repel and resist by force of arms as well by sea as by
land, and by all fitting ways and means whatsoever all such person and
persons as shall at any time hereafter attempt or enterprise the destruction, invasion, detriment or annoyance to the said plantation or inh9itants
. . . Nevertheless . . . if any . . . persons . . . of the said company or plantation . . . shall . . . rob or spoil by sea or land . . . any of the subjects of
any prince or state being then in league and amity with us, . . . we . . .
shall make open proclamation . . . that the . . . persons having committed
any such robbery or spoil, shall . . . make full restitution or satisfaction of
all such injuries done, ...

The English Puritans who settled in New England developed a
land system which permitted group settlement, and helped to
maintain their socio-religious cohesiveness. This selection is
a description of that system by Edward Johnson who helped to
establish Woburn, Massachusetts.
(Source: J. Franklin Jameson, ed., Johnson's Wonder-Working
Providence, New York, 1910.)

But to begin, this Town, as all others, had its bounds fixed by the
General Court, to the contenese   contents   of four miles square, (beginning at the end of Charles Town bounds).   The grant is to seven men of
good and honest report, upon condition, that within two year they erect
houses for habitation thereon, and so go on to make a Town thereof, upon
the Act of Court; these seven men have power to give and grant out lands
unto any persons who are willing to take up their dwellings within the said
precinct, and to be admitted to al common priviledges of the said Town,
giving them such an ample portion, both of Medow and Upland, as their
present and future stock of cattel and hands were like to improve, with
eye had to others that might after come to populate the said Town; this they
did without any respect of persons, yet such as were exorbitant, and of a
turbulent spirit, unfit for a civil society, they would reject, till they come to
mend their manners; such came not to enjoy any freehold.   These seven
men ordered and disposed of the streets of the Town, as might be best for
improvement of the Land, and yet civil and religious society maintained;
to which end those that had land neerest the place for Sabbath Assembly, had
a lesser quantity at home, and more farther off to improve for corn, of all
kinds; they refused not men for their poverty, but according to their ability were helpful to the poorest sort, in building their houses, and distributed
to them land accordingly; the poorest had six or seven acres of Medow, and
twenty five of Upland, or thereabouts.   Thus was this Town populated, to
the number of sixty families, or thereabout, and after this manner are the
Towns of New England peopled.   The scituation of this Town is in the highest part of the yet peopled land, neere upon the headsprings of many
considerable rivers, or their branches, as the first rise of Ipswitch river,
and the rise of Shasin river, one of the most considerable branches of
Merrimeck, as also the first rise of Mistick river and ponds, it is very
full of pleasant springs, and great variety of very good water, which the
Summers heat causeth to be more cooler, and the Winters cold maketh more
warmer; their Medows are not large, but lye in divers places to particular
dwellings, the like doth their Springs; their Land is very fruitful in many
places, although they have no great quantity of plain land in any one place
yet doth their Rocks and Swamps yeeld very good food for cattel; as also
they have Mast and Tar for shipping, but the distance of place by land causeth them as yet to be unprofitable; they have great store of iron ore; their
meeting-house stands in a small Plain, where four streets meet; the people
are very laborious, if not exceeding some of them.

Now to declare how this people proceeded in religious matters and so consequently all the Churches of Christ planted in New England, when they came once to hopes of being such a competent number of people, as might be able to maintain a Minister, they then surely seated themselves, and not before, it being as unnatural for a right N. E. man to live without an able Ministery, as for a Smith to work his iron without a fire . . . .

The reasons motivating Englishmen to come to America were as varied as the men themselves. This selection, written by John Winthrop, the first governor of Massachusetts, attempts to explain why the English Puritans emigrated.
(Source: John Winthrop, "Considerations," Old South Leaflets, no. 50, pp. 4-11.)

REASONS TO BE CONSIDERED FOR JUSTIFYING THE UNDERTAKERS OF THE INTENDED PLANTATION IN NEW ENGLAND AND FOR ENCOURAGING SUCH WHOSE HEARTS GOD SHALL MOVE TO JOIN WITH THEM IN IT.

1. It will be a service to the church of great consequence to carry the gospel into those parts of the world, to help on the coming in of fullness of the Gentiles and to raise a bulwark against the kingdom of Antichrist, which the Jesuits labor to rear up in those parts.

2. All other churches of Europe are brought to desolation and our sins for which the Lord begins already to frown upon us, do threaten us fearfully; and who knows but that God hath provided this place to be a refuge for many whom He means to save out of the general calamity, and seeing the church hath no place left to fly into but the wilderness, what better work can there be than to go before and provide tabernacles and food for her against she cometh thither.

3. This land grows weary of her inhabitants, so as man who is the most precious of all creatures is here more vile and base than the earth we tread upon and of less price among us than a horse or a sheep. Masters are forced by authority to entertain servants, parents to maintain their own children. All towns complain of the burdens of their poor though we have taken up many unnecessary, yea unlawful, trades to maintain them. And we use the authority of the law to hinder the increase of people as urging the execution of the state against cottages and inmates; and thus it is come to pass that children, servants, and neighbors (especially if they be poor) are counted the greatest burden which, if things were right, it would be the chiefest earthly blessing.

4. The whole earth is the Lord's garden and He hath given it to the sons of men with a general commission (Gen. 1:28): Increase and multiply, replenish the earth and subdue it, which was again renewed to Noah; the end is double, moral and natural, that man might enjoy the fruits of the earth and God might have His due glory from the creature. Why, then, should we stand here striving for places of habitation (many men spending as much labor and cost to recover or keep sometimes an acre or two of land as would procure them many hundred as good or better in another country) and in the meantime suffer a whole continent as fruitful and convenient for the use of man to lie waste without any improvement?

5. We are grown to that height of intemperance in all excess of riot as no man's estate almost will suffice to keep sail with his equals, and he who fails herein must live in scorn and contempt; hence it comes that all arts and trades are carried in that deceitful and unrighteous course as it is almost impossible for a good and upright man to maintain his charge and live comfortably in any of them.

6. The fountains of learning and religion are so corrupted as (beside the unsupportable charge of the education) most children (even the best wits and fairest hopes) are perverted, corrupted, and utterly overthrown by the multitude of evil examples and the licentious government of those seminaries where men strain at gnats and swallow camels, use all severity for maintenance of caps and other accomplements   accomplishments but suffer all ruffian-like fashion and disorder to manners to pass uncontrolled.

7. What can be a better work and more honorable and worthy a Christian than to help raise and support a particular church while it is in the infancy and to join his forces with such a company of faithful people as by a timely assistance may grow strong and prosper, and for want of it may be put to great hazard, if not wholly ruined?

8. If any such who are known to be godly and live in wealth and prosperity here shall forsake all this to join themselves to this church and to run a hazard with them of a hard and mean condition, it will be an example of great use both for removing the scandal of worldly and sinister respects which is cast upon the adventurers, to give more life to the faith of God's people in their prayers for the plantation, and to encourage others to join the more willingly in it.

9. It appears to be a work of God for the good of His church in that He hath disposed the hearts of so many of His wise and faithful servants (both ministers and others) not only to approve the enterprise but to interest themselves in it, some in their persons and estates, others by their serious advice and help otherwise, and all by their prayers for the welfare of it.   Amos 3:   The Lord revealeth His secrets to His servants the prophets.   It is likely He hath some great work in hand which He hath stirred up to encourage His servants to this plantation, for He doth not use to seduce His people by His own prophets but commits that office to the ministry of false prophets and lying spirits.

DIVERSE OBJECTIONS WHICH HAVE BEEN MADE AGAINST THIS PLANTATION WITH THEIR ANSWERS AND RESOLUTIONS.

Objection 1.   We have no warrant to enter upon that land which hath been so long possessed by others.

Answer 1.   That which lies common and hath never been replenished or subdued is free to any that will possess and improve it, for God hath given to the sons of men a double right to the earth.   There is a natural right and a civil right.   The first right was natural when man held the earth in common, every man sowing and feeding where he pleased.   And then as men and the cattle increased, they appropriated certain parcels of ground by enclosing and peculiar manurance occupancy . And this in time gave them a civil right. Such was the right which Ephron the Hittite had in the field of Mackpelah, wherein Abraham could not bury a dead corpse without leave, though for the out parts of the country, which lay common, he dwelt upon them and took the fruit of them at his pleasure. The like did Jacob, which fed his cattle as bold in Hamor's land (for he is said to be the lord of the country), and other places where he came, as the native inhabitants themselves. And that in those times and places men accounted nothing their own but that which they had appropriated by their own industry appears plainly by this: that Abimelech's servants in their own country when they oft contended with Isaac's servants about wells which they had digged yet never strove for the land wherein they were. So likewise between Jacob and Laban-he would not take a kid of Laban's without his special contract, but he makes no bargain with him for the land where they feed; and it is very probable if the country had not been as free for Jacob as for Laban, that covetous wretch would have made his advantage of it and have upbraided Jacob with it, as he did with his cattle. And for the natives in New England; they enclose no land, neither have any settled habitation, nor any tame cattle to improve the land by, and so have no other but a natural right to those countries. So as if we leave them sufficient for their use we may lawfully take the rest, there being more than enough for them and us.

2. We shall come in with the good leave of the natives, who find benefit already by our neighborhood and learn of us to improve part to more use than before they could do the whole, and by this means we come in by valuable purchase. For they have of us that which will yield them more benefit than all the land which we h0e from them.

3. God hath consumed the natives with a great plague in those parts so as there be few inhabitants left.

Objection 2. It will be a great wrong to our church to take away the good people, and we shall lay it the more open to the judgment feared.

Answer 1. The departing of good people from a country doth not cause a judgment but foreshows it, which may occasion such as remain to turn from their evil ways that they may prevent it or to take some other course that they may escape it.

2. Such as go away are of no observation in respects of those who remain, and they are likely to do more good there than here; and since Christ's time, the church is to be considered as universal without distinction of countries, so as he who doeth good in any one place serves the church in all places in regard of the unity.

3. It is the revealed will of God that the Gospel should be preached to all nations, and though we know not whether those barbarians will receive it at first or not, yet it is a good work to serve God's providence in offering it to them. And this is fittest to be done by God's own servants, for God shall have glory by it, though they refuse it, and there is good hope that the posterity shall by this means be gathered into Christ's sheepfold.

Objection 3.   We have feared a judgment a great while, but yet we are safe; it were better therefore to stay till it come, and either we may fly then or if we be overtaken in it we may well content ourselves to suffer with such a church as ours is.

Answer.   It is likely this consideration made the churches beyond the seas, as the Palatinate, Rochelle, etc., to sit still at home and not to look out for shelter while they might have found it, but the woeful spectacle of their ruin may teach us more wisdom to avoid the plague when it is foreseen and not to tarry as they did till it overtake us.   If they were now at their former liberty, we might be sure they would take other courses for their safety; and though half of them had miscarried in their escape, yet had it not be so miserable to themselves nor scandalous to relition as this desperate backsliding and abjuring the truth which many of the ancient professors among them and the whole posterity which remain are now plagued into.

Objection 4   The ill success of other plantations may tell us what will become of this.

Answer 1.   None of the former sustained any great damage but Virginia, which happened through their own sloth and security.

2.   The argument is not good, for thus it stands: some plantations have miscarried, therefore we should not make any.   It consists in particulars and so concludes nothing.   We might as well reason thus: many houses have been burnt by kilns, therefore we should use none; many ships have been cast away, therefore we should content ourselves with our home commodities and not adventure men's lives at sea for those things which we might live without; some men have been undone by being advanced to great places, therefore we should refuse our preferment, etc.

3.   The fruit of any public design is not to be discerned by the immediate success.   It may appear in time that former plantations were all to good use.

4.   There were great and fundamental errors in the former which are like to be avoided in this.   For first their main end was carnal and not religious.   Secondly, they used unfit instruments, a multitude of rude and misgoverned persons, the very scum of the people.   Thirdly, they did not establish a right form of government. . . .

The Maryland Charter, an excellent example of a proprietary
grant, remained the prototype for such charters for many years.
The political provisions of the charter, which the English settlers
were bound to abide by, are covered here.
(Source: Francis Newton Thorpe, comp. and ed., The Federal
and State Constitutions, Colonial Charters, and other Organic
Laws of the States, Territories, and Colonies Now Forming the
United States of America, III, Washington, Government Printing
Office, 1909.)

V.   And we do by these Presents, for us, our Heirs, and Successors,
Make, Create, and Constitute Him, the now Baron of Baltimore, and his
Heirs, the true and absolute Lords and Proprietaries of the Region aforesaid, and of all other Premises (except the before excepted) saving always
the Faith and Allegiance and Sovereign Dominion due to Us, our Heirs, and
Successors; to have, hold, possess, and enjoy the aforesaid Region, Islands,
Islets, and other the Premises, unto the aforesaid now Baron of Baltimore,
and to his Heirs and Assigns, to the sole and proper Behoof and Use of him,
the now Baron of Baltimore, his Heirs and Assigns, forever.   To Hold
of Us, our Heirs and Successors, Kings of England, as of our Castle of
Windsor, in our County of Berks, in free and common Soccage, by Fealty
only for all Services, and not in Capite, nor by Knight's Service, Yielding
therefore unto Us, our Heirs and Successors Two Indian Arrows of these
Parts, to be delivered at the said Castle of Windsor, every Year, on Tues-
day in Easter Week: And also the fifth part of all Gold and Silver Ore,
which shall happen from Time to Time, to be found within the aforesaid
Limits.
VI.   Now, That the aforesaid Region, thus by us granted and described, may be eminently distinguished above all other Regions of that
Territory, and decorated with more 0ple Titles, Know Ye, that We, of
our more especial Grace, certain knowledge, and mere Motion, have
thought fit that the said Region and Islands be erected into a Province,
as out of the Plenitude of our royal Power and Prerogative, We do, for
Us, our Heirs and Successors, erect and incorporate the same into a Province, and nominate the same Maryland, by which Name We will that it
shall from henceforth be called.
VII.   And forasmuch as We have above made and ordained the aforesaid now Baron of Baltimore, the true Lord and Proprietary of the whole
Province aforesaid, Know Ye therefore further, that We, for Us, our
Heirs and Successors, do grant unto the said now Baron, (in whose Fidel-
ity, Prudence, Justice, and provident Circumspection of Mind, We re-
pose the greatest Confidence) and to his Heirs, for the good and happy
Government of the said Province, free, full, and absolute Power, by the
Tenor of these Presents, to Ordain, Make, and Enact Laws, of what Kind
soever, according to their sound Discretions, whether relating to the
Public State of said Province, or the private Utility of Individuals, of and

with the Advice, Assent, and Approbation of the Free-Men of the same Province, or the greater Part of them, or of their Delegates or Deputies, whom
We will shall be called together for the framing of Laws, when, and as often
as Need shall require, by the aforesaid now Baron of Baltimore, and his
Heirs, and in the Form which shall seem best to him or them, and the same
to publish under the Seal of the aforesaid now Baron of Baltimore, and his
Heirs, and duly to execute the same upon all Persons, for the time being,
within the aforesaid Province, and the Limits thereof, or under his or
their Government and Power, in Sailing towards Maryland, or thence Returning, Outward-bound, either to England, or elsewhere, whether to ky
other Part of Our, or of ky foreign Dominions, wheresoever established, by
the Imposition of Fines, Imprisonment and other Punishment whatsoever;
even if it be necessary, and the Quality of the Offence require it, by Priva-
tion of Member, or Life, by him the aforesaid now Baron of Baltimore, and
his Heirs, or by his or their Deputy, Lieutenant, Judges, Justices, Magistrates, Officers, and Ministers, to be constituted and appointed according
to the Tenor and true Intent of these Presents, and to constitute and ordain
Judges, Justices Magistrates, and Officers of what kind, for what Cuse,
and with what Power soever, within that Land, and the Sea of those Parts,
in such form as to the said now Baron of Baltimore, or his Heirs, shall
seem most fitting; And also to Remit, Release, Pardon, and Abolish, all
Crimes and Offences whatsoever against such Laws, whether before, or
after Judgment passed; and to do all and singular other Things belonging
to the Completion of Justice, and to Courts, Praetorian Judicatories, and
Tribunals, Judical Forms and Modes of Proceeding, although express
Mention thereof in these Presents be not made; and, by Judges by them del-
egated, to award Process, hold Pleu, and determine in those Courst,
Praetorian: Which said Laws, so to be published as above-said, We will
enjoin, charge, and command, to be most absolute and firm in Law, and to
be Kept in those Parts by all the Subjects and Liege-Men of Us, our Heirs,
and Successors, so far as they concern them, and to be inviolably observed
under the Penalties therein expressed, or to be expressed.   So, nevertheless, that the Laws aforesaid be consonant to Reason, and be not repugnant
or contrary, but (so far as conveniently may be) agreeable to the Laws,
Statutes, Customs, and Rights of this Our Kingdom of England.

   VIII.   And forasmuch as, in the Government of so great a Province,
sudden accidents may frequently happen, to which it will be necessary
to apply a Remedy, before the Freeholders of the said Province, their
Delegates, or Deputies, can be called together for the framing of Laws
neither will it be fit that so great a Number of People should immediately,
on such emergent Occasion, be called together, We therefore, for the
better Government of so great a Province, do Will and Ordain, and by
these Presents, for Us, our Heirs and Successors, do grant unto the said
now Baron of Baltimore, and to his Heirs, by themselves or by their Magistrates and Officers, thereunto duly to be constituted as aforesaid, as well
for the Conservation of the Peace, as for the better Government of the
People inhabiting therein, and publicly to notify the same to all Persons
whom the same in any wise do or may affect.   Which Ordinances we will

to be invioably observed within the said Province, under the Pains to be expressed in the same. So that the said Ordinances be consonant to Reason and be not repugnant or contrary, but (so far as conveniently may be done) agreeable to the Laws, Statutes, or Rights of our Kingdom of England: And so that the same Ordinances do not, in any Sort, extend to oblige, bind, charge, or take away the Right or Interest of any Person or Persons, of, or in Member, Life, Freehold, Goods or Chattels . . . . . .

X. We will also, and of our more abundant Grace, for Us, our Heirs and Successors, do firmly charge, constitute, ordain, and command, that the said Provinee by of our Allegiance; and that all and singular the subjects and Liege-Men of Us, our Heirs and Successors, transplanted, or hereafter to be transplanted into the Province aforesaid, and the Children of them, and of others their Descendants, whether already born there, or hereafter to be born, be and shall be Natives and Liege-Men of Us, our Heirs and Successors, of our Kingdom of England and Ireland; and in all Things shall be held, treated, reputed, and esteemed as the faithful Liege-Men of Us, and our Heirs and Successors, born within our Kingdom of England; also Lands, Tenements, Revenues, Services, and other Hereditaments whatsoever, within our Kingdom of England; also Lands, Tenements, Revenues, Services, and other Hereditaments whatsoever, within our Kingdom of England, and other our Dominions, to inherit, or otherwise purchase, receive, take, have, hold, buy, and possess, and the same to use and enjoy, and the same to give, sell, alien and bequeth; and likewise all Privileges, Franchises and Liberties of this our Kingdom of England, freely, quietly, and peaceably to have and possess, and the same may use and enjoy in the same manner as our Liege-Men born, or to be born within our said Kingdom of England, without Impediment, Molestation, Vexation, Impeachment, or Grievance of Us, or any of our Heirs or Successors; any Statute, Act, Ordinance, or Provision to the contrary thereof, notwithstanding . . . .

In 1639, the various groups of English settlers along the Connecti-
cut River, took the initiative, and set up their own government.
This selection is a portion of the constitution they created.
(Source: B. P. Poore, compiler, Federal and State Constitutions,
Part I, Washington, 1878.)

Forasmuch as it hath pleased the Almighty God by the wise disposition of his divine providence so to order and dispose of things that we the
inhabitants and residents of Windsor, Hartford and Wethersfield are now
cohabiting and dwelling in and upon the River of Connecticut and the lands
thereunto adjoining; and well knowing where a people are gathered together
the word of God requires that to maintain the peace and union of such a people there should be an orderly and decent government established according to God, to order and dispose of the affairs of the people at all seasons
as occasion shall require: do therefore associate and conjoin ourselves
to be as one public state of commonwealth; and do, for ourselves and our
successors and such as shall be adjoined to us at any time hereafter, enter
into combination and confederation together, to maintain and preserve
liberty and purity of the gospel of our Lord Jesus, which we now profess
as also the discipline of the churches, which according to the truth of the
said gospel is now practised amongst us; as also in our civil affairs to
be guided and governed according to such laws, rules, orders and decrees
as shall be made, ordered and decreed, as followeth:
1. It is ordered, sentenced and decreed, that there shall be yearly
two general assemblies or courts, the one the second Thursday in April,
the other the second Thursday in September, following; the first shall be
called the Court of Election, wherein shall be yearly chosen . . . so many
magistrates and other public officers as shall be found requisite: whereof
one to be chosen governor for the year ensuing . . . (and no other magistrate to be chosen for more than one year), provided always there be six
chosen beside the governor; which being chosen and sworn . . . shall have
power to administer justice according to the laws here established, and
for want thereof according to the rule of the word of God; which choice
shall be made by all that are admitted freemen and have taken the oath of
fidelity, and do cohabit within this jurisdiction (having been admitted inhabitants by the major part of the town wherein they live) or the major
part of such as shall be then present.
2. It is ordered, sentenced and decreed, that the election of the
aforesaid magistrates shall be on this manner. Every person present and
qualified for choice shall bring in (to the persons deputed to receive them)
one single paper with the name of him written in it whom he desires to have
governor, and he that hath the greatest number of papers shall be governor,
for that year. And the rest of the magistrates or public officers to be
chosen in this manner: The secretary . . . shall first read the names of
all that are to be put to choice and then shall severally nominate them distinctly, and every one that would have the person nominated to be chosen

shall bring in one single paper written upon, and he that would not have him chosen shall bring in a blank. And every one that hath more written papers than blanks shall be a magistrate for that year . . . . But in case there should not be six chosen as aforesaid, beside the governor . . . then he or they which have the most written papers shall be a magistrate or magistrates for the ensuing year, to make up the aforesaid number.

3. It is ordered, sentenced and decreed, that the secretary shall not nominate any person . . . which was not propounded in some General Court before, to be nominated the next election; and to that end it shall be lawful for each of the towns aforesaid by their deputies to nominate any two who they conceive fit to be put to election; and the Court may add so many more as they judge requisite.

4. It is ordered, sentenced and decreed, that no person be chosen governor above once in two years, and that the governor be always a member of some approved congregation, and formerly of the magistracy within this jurisdiction; and all the magistrates freemen of this Commonwealth: and that no magistrate or other public officer shall execute any part of his or their office before they are severally sworn . . . .

5. It is ordered, sentenced, and decreed, that to the aforesaid court of election the several towns shall send their deputies, and when the elections are ended they may proceed in any public service as at other courts. Also the other General Court in September shall be for making of laws, and any other public occasion, which concerns the good of the Commonwealth.

6. It is ordered, sentenced and decreed, thw the governor shall . . . send out summons to the constables of every town for the calling of these two standing courts, one month at least before their several times. And also if the governor and the greatest part of the magistrates see cause upon any special occasion to call a General Court, they may give order to the secretary so to do within fourteen days warning; and if urgent necessity so require, upon a shorter notice, giving sufficient grounds for it to the deputies when they meet, or else be questioned for the same. And if the governor and major part of magistrates shall either neglect or refuse to call the two General standing Courts . . . , as also at other times when the occasions of the Commonwealth require, the freemen thereof, or the major part of them, shall petition to them so to do. If then it be either denied or neglected the said freemen . . . shall have power to give order to the constables of the several towns to do the same, and so may meet together, and choose to themselves a moderator, and may proceed to do any act of power, which any other General Court may.

7. It is ordered, sentenced and decreed, that after there are warrants given out for any of the said General Courts, the constable or constables of each town shall forthwith give notice distinctly to the inhabitants of the same, in some public assembly or by going or sending from house to house, that at a place and time by him or them limited and set, they meet and assemble themselves together to elect and choose certain deputies to be at the General Court then following to agitate the affairs of the Commonwealth; which said deputies shall be chosen by all that are admitted inhabitants in the several towns and have taken the oath of fidelity; provided that none be

chosen a deputy for any General Court which is not a freeman of this Commonwealth . . .

8. It is ordered, sentenced and decreed, that Windsor, Hartford, and Wethersfield shall have power, each town, to send four of their freemen as deputies to every General Court; and whatsoever other towns shall be hereafter added to this jurisdiction, they shall send so many deputies as the Court shall judge meet, a reasonable proportion to the number of freemen that are in the said towns being to be attended therein; which deputies shall have the power of the whole town to give their votes and allowance to all such laws and orders as may be for the public good, and unto which the said towns are to be bound.

9. It is ordered and decreed, that the deputies thus chosen shall have power and liberty to appoint a time and a place of meeting together before any General Court to advise and consult of all such things as may concern the good of the public, as also to examine their own elections . . . and if they or the greatest part of them find any election to be illegal they may seclude such for present from their meeting, and return the same and their reasons to the Court. And if it prove true, the Court may fine the party or parties so intruding and the town . . . and give out a warrant to go to a new election in a legal way . . . . Also the said deputies shall have power to fine any that shall be disorderly at their meetings, or for not coming in due time or place according to appointment . . . .

10. It is ordered, sentenced and decreed, that every General Court (except such as through neglect of the governor and the greatest part of magistrates the freemen themselves do call) shall consist of the governor, or some one chosen to moderate the Court, and four other magistrates at least, with the major part of the deputies of the several towns legally chosen. And in case the freemen or major part of them, through neglect or refusal of the governor and . . . the magistrates, shall call a Court, it shall consist of the major part of freemen that are present or their deputies, with a moderator chosen by them. In which said General Courts shall consist the supreme power of the Commonwealth, and they only shall have power to make laws or repeal them, to grant levies, to admit of freemen, dispose of lands . . . , and also shall have power to call either Court or magistrate or any other person whatsoever into question for any misdemeanor, and may for just causes displace or deal otherwise according to the nature of the offense; and also may deal in any other matter that concerns the good of this Commonwealth, except election of magistrates, which shall be done by the whole body of freemen.

In which Court the governor or moderator shall have power to order the Court to give liberty of speech, and silence unseasonable and disorderly speakings, to put all things to vote, and in case the vote be equal to have the casting voice. But none of these Courts shall be adjourned or dissolved without the consent of the major part of the Court.

11. It is ordered, sentenced and decreed, that when any General Court upon the occasions of the Commonwealth have agreed upon any sum . . . . to be levied upon the several towns within this jurisdiction, that a committee be chosen to set out and appoint what shall be the proportion of every town to pay . . . , provided the committees be made up of an equal number out of each town.

The following selection was written by John Hammond, who had
come to America in 1635. In it, he gave some very good advice to
those English emigrants who intended to come to the New World
as indentured servants.
(Source: John Hammond, Leah and Rachel . . . . ., 1656, in
Peter Force, ed., Tracts and Other Papers. . . ., 4 vols., No. 14,
1835-1846.)

Let such as are so minded [to come to America]   not rashly throw
themselves upon the voyage, but observe the nature, and inquire the qualities
of the persons with whom they engage to transport themselves; or if , as not
acquainted with such as inhabit there, but go with merchants and mariners,
who transport them to others, let their covenant be such that after their
arrival they have a fortnight's time assigned them to inquire of their master
and make choice of such as they intend to expire their time with, nor let
that brand of selling of servants be any discouragement to deter any from
going.   For if a time must be served, it is all one with whom it be served,
provided they be people of honest repute, with which the country is well
replenished.

And be sure to have your contract in writing and under hand and seal,
for if ye go over upon promise made to do this or that, or to be free or your
own men, it signifies nothing, for by a law of the country (waiving all promises) anyone coming in, and not paying their own passages, must serve, if
men or women, four years; if younger, according to their years, but where
an indenture is, that is binding and observing.

The usual allowance for servants is (besides their charge of passage
defrayed), at their expiration a year's provision of corn, double apparel,
tools necessary, and land according to the custom of the country, which is an
old delusion, for there is no land customarily due to the servant, but to
the master, and therefore that servant is unwise that will not dash out that
custom in his covenant, and make that due of land absolutely his own; which
although at the present not of so great consequence, yet in few years will
be of much worth, as I shall hereafter make manifest.

When ye go aboard, expect the ship somewhat troubled and in a hurly-
burly until ye clear the land's end; and that the ship is rummaged, and things
not put to rights, which many times discourages the passengers and
makes them wish the voyage unattempted.   But this is but for a short season
and washes off when at sea, where the time is pleasantly passed away,
though not with such choice plenty as the shore affords . . . .

The labor servants are put to is not so hard nor of such continuance
as husbandmen nor handicraftsmen are kept at in England . . . . Little or
nothing is done in winter time; none ever work before sun rising nor after
sun set; in the summer they rest, sleep, or exercise themselves five hours
in the heat of the day.   Saturday's afternoon is always their own, the old
holidays are observed, and the Sabbath spent in good exercises.

103

The women are not (as is reported) put into the ground work, but occupy such domestic employments and housewifery as in England, that is, dressing victuals, righting up the house, milking, employed about dairies, washing, sewing, etc.; and both men and women have times of recreations, as much or more than in any part of the world besides. Yet some wenches that are nasty, beastly, and not fit to be so employed are put into the ground, for reason tells us they must not at charge be transported and then maintained for nothing, but those that prove to awkward are rather burdensome than servants desirable or useful . . . .

Those servants that will be industrious may in their time of service gain a competent estate before their freedoms, which is usually done by many, and they gain esteem and assistance that appear so industrious. There is no master almost but will allow his servant a parcel of clear ground to plant some tobacco in for himself, which he may husband at those many idle times he hath allowed him and not prejudice, but rejoice, his master to see it; which in time of shipping he may lay out for commodities, and in summer sell them again with advantage, and get a sow-pig or two, which anybody almost will give him; and his master suffer him to keep them with his own, which will be no charge to his master, and with one year's increase of them may purchase a cow-calf or two, and by that time he is for himself. He may have cattle, hogs, and tobacco of his own, and come to live gallantly; but this must be gained (as I said) by industry and affability, not by sloth nor churlish behavior . . . .

It is known (such preferment hath this country rewarded the industrious with) that some from being wool-hoppers and of as mean and meaner employment in England have there grown great merchants and attained to the most eminent advancements the country afforded. If men cannot gain (by diligence) it will hardly be done (unless by mere luck as gamesters thrive and other accidental states) in those parts [or] in any part whatsoever. I speak not only mine own opinion but divers others and something by experience.

Recruitment propaganda was always an important way of getting new English immigrants to come to America. The two selec-' tions cited here provide good examples of this type of advertising. The first appeal came from a former Maryland indentured servant, George Alsop; and the second, from the proprietors of the Carolina colonies.

(Source: N. D. Mereness, ed., George Alsop, A Character of the Province of Maryland, Cleveland, 1902; B. R. Carroll, ed., Historical Collections of South Carolina; Embracing Many Rare and Valuable Pamphlets, and Other Documents, II, New York, 1836.)

The three main commodities this country affords for traffic are tobacco, furs and flesh. Furs and skins, as beavers, otters, muskrats, raccoons, wildcats, and elk or buffalo, with divers others, which were first made vendible by the Indians of the country, and sold to the inhabitants, and by them to the merchant, and so transported into England and other places where it becomes most commodious.

Tobacco is the only solid staple commodity of this province. The use of it was first found out by the Indians many ages ago, and transferred into Christendom by that great discoverer of America, Columbus. It is generally made by all the inhabitants of this province; and between the months of March and April they sow the seed . . . in small beds and patches dug up and made so by art. About May the plants commonly appear green in those beds. In June they are transplanted from their beds, and set in little hillocks in distant rows, dug up for the same purpose. Some twice or thrice they are weeded, and succored from their illegitimate leaves that would be peeping out from the body of the stalk. They top the several plants as they find occasion in their predominating rankness. About the middle of September they cut the tobacco down, and carry it into houses (made for that purpose) to bring it to its purity; and after it has attained, by a convenient attendance upon time, to its perfection, it is then tied up in bundles and packed into hogsheads, and then laid by for the trade.

Between November and January there arrives in this province shipping to the number of twenty sail and upwards, all merchantmen laden with commodities to traffic and dispose of, trucking with the planter for silks, Hollands, serges and broadcloths, with other necessary goods, prized at such and such rates as shall be judged on is fair and legal, for tobacco at so much the pound, and advantage on both sides considered:---the planter for his work, and the merchant for adventuring himself and his commodity into so far a country. Thus is the trade on both sides driven with a fair and honest decorum.

The inhabitants of this province are seldom or never put to the affrightment of being robbed of their money, nor to dirty their fingers by telling of vast sums. They have more bags to carry corn, than coin . . .

105

The very effects of the dirt of this province afford as great a profit to the general inhabitant as the gold of Peru does to the straight-breeched commonalty of the Spaniard.

Our shops and exchanges of Maryland are the merchants' storehouses', where with few words and protestations goods are bought and delivered; not like those shopkeepers' boys in London that continually cry, "What do ye lack, sir? What do ye buy?" yelping with so wide a mouth, as if some apothecary had hired their mouths to stand open to catch gnats and vagabond flies in.

Tobacco is the current coin of Maryland and will sooner purchase commodities from the merchant, than money. I must confess the New England men that trade into this province had rather have fat pork for their goods than tobacco or furs, which I conceive is, because their bodies being fast bound up with the cords of restringent zeal, they are fain to make use of the lineaments of this non-Canaanite creature physically to loosen them; for a bit of a pound on a two-penny rye loaf, according to the original receipt, will bring the costiv'st red-eared zealot in some three hours' time to a fine stool, if methodically observed.

Madeira wines, sugars, salt, wicker chairs and tin candlesticks are the most of the commodities they bring in. They arrive in Maryland about September, being most of them ketches and barks and such small vessels, and those disperse themselves into several small creeks of this province to sell and dispose of their commodities, where they know the market is most fit for their small adventures.

CAROLINAS

Is there therefore any younger Brother who is born of Gentile blood and whose Spirit is elevated above the common sort, and yet the hard usage of our Country hath not allowed suitable fortune; he will not surely be afraid to leave his Native Soil to advance his Fortunes equal to his Blood and Spirit, and so he will avoid those unlawful ways too many of our young Gentlemen take to maintain themselves according to their high education, having but small Estates; here, with a few Servants and a small Stock a great Estate may be raised, although his Birth have not entitled him to any of the Land of his Ancestors, yet his Industry may supply him so, as to make him the head of as famous a family.

Such as are here tormented with much care how to get worth to gain a Livelyhood, or that with their labour can hardly get a comfortable subsistance, shall do well to go to this place, where any man what-ever, that is but willing to take moderate pains, may be assured of a most comfortable subsistance, and be in a way to raise his fortunes far beyond what he could ever hope for in England. Let no man be troubled at the thoughts of being a Servant for 4 or 5 year, for I can assure you, that many men give money with their children to serve 7 years, to take more pains and fare nothing so well as the Servants in this Plantation will do. Then it is to be considered, that so soon as he is out of his time, he hath Land and Tools, and Clothes given him, and is in a way of advancement. Therefore all Artificers, as

Carpenters, Wheel-rights, Joyners, Coopers, Brick-layers, Smiths, or diligent Husbandmen and Labourers, that are willing to advance their fortunes, and live in a most pleasant healthful and fruitful Country, where Artificers are of high esteem, and used with all Civility and Courtesie imaginable, may take notice . . . . . .

If any Maid or single Woman have a desire to go over, they will think themselves in the Golden Age, when Men paid a Dowry for their Wives; for if they be but Civil, and under 50 years of Age, some honest Man or other, will purchase them for their Wives.

Printed descriptions of the New World, designed for English readers, praised conditions in America, and provided information to encourage emigration. This was true of the following selection.
(Source: Daniel Denton, A Brief Description of New York, London, 1670.)

I may say, and say truly, that if there be any terrestrial happiness to be had by people of all ranks, especially of an inferior rank, it must certainly be here: here any one may furnish himself with land, and live rent-free, yea with such a quantity of land, that he may weary himself with walking over his fields of Corn, and all sorts of Grain: and let his stock of Cattel amount to some hundreds, he needs not fear their want of pasture in the Summer, or Fodder in the Winter, the Woods affording sufficient supply. For the Summer season, where you have grass as high as a mans knees, nay, as high as his waste, interlaced with Pea-vines and other weeds that Cattel much delight in, as much as a man can press thorough; and these woods also every mile or half-mile are furnished with fresh ponds, brooks, or rivers,. . . .: Here those which Fortune hath frown'd upon in England, to deny them an inheritance amongst their Brethren, or such as by their utmost labors can scarcely procure a living, I say such may procure here inheritances of lands and possessions, stock themselves with all sorts of Cattel, enjoy the benefit of them whilst they live, and leave them to the benefit of their children when they die: Here you need not trouble the shambles for meat, nor Bakers and Brewers for Beer and Bread, nor run to a Linnen-Draper for a supply, every one making their own Linnen, and a great part of their woolen cloth for their ordinary wearing: And how prodigal, if I may so say, hath Nature been to furnish the Countrey with all sorts of wilde Beasts and Fowle, which every one hath an interest in, and may hunt at his pleasure; where besides the pleasure in hunting, he may furnish his house with excellent fat Venison, Turkies, Geese, Heath-Hens, Cranes, Swans, Ducks, Pidgeons, and the like: and wearied with that he may go a Fishing, where the Rivers are so furnished, that he may supply himself with Fish before he can leave off the Recreation: where you may travel . . . from one end of the Countrey to another, with as much security as if you were lockt within your own Chamber; And if you chance to meet with an Indian-Town, they shall give you the best entertainment they have, and upon your desire, direct you on your way: But that which adds happiness to all the rest, is the Healthfulness of the place, where many people in twenty years time never know what sickness is: . . . where besides the sweetness of the Air, the Countrey it self sends forth such a fragrant smell, that it may be perceived at Sea before they can make the Land: where no evil fog or vapour doth no sooner appear, but a North-west or Westerly winde doth immediately dissolve it, and drive it away: What shall I say more? you shall scarce see a house, but the South side is begirt with Hives of Bees, which increase after an incredible manner: That I must needs say, that if there be any terrestrial Canaan, 'tis surely here, where the land floweth with milk and honey.

William Penn, the proprietor of Pennsylvania, also advertised for emigrants. His first appeals were designed for English settlers, and did bare some results as witnessed by the medley of English social groups who came to his colony.

(Source: "Some Account of the Province of Pennsylvania in America . . . ." in Samuel Hazard, ed., The Register of Pennsylvania, I, Philadelphia, 1828.)

1st. Industrious husbandmen and day-labourers, that are hardly able (with extreme labour) to maintain their families and portion their children.

2dly. Laborious handicrafts, especially carpenters, masons, smiths, weavers, taylors, tanners, shoemakers, shipwrights, &c. where they may be spared or low in the world; and as they shall want no encouragement, so their labour is worth more there than here, and there provision cheaper.

3rdly. A plantation seems a fit place for those ingenious spirits that being low in the world, are much clogg'd and oppres'd about a livelyhood, for the means of subsisting being easie there, they may have time and opportunity to gratify their inclinations, and thereby improve science and help nurseries of people.

4thly. A fourth sort of men to whom a plantation would be proper, takes in those that are younger brothers of small inheritances; yet because they would live in sight of their kindred in some proportion to their quality, and can't do it without a labour that looks like farming, their condition is too strait for them; and if married, their children are aften too numerous for the estate, and are frequently bred up to no trades, but are a kind of hangers on or retainers to the elder brothers table and charity: which is a mischief, as in it self to be lamented, so here to be remedied; for land they have for next to nothing, which with moderate labour produces plenty of all things necessary for life, and such an increase as by traffique may supply them with all conveniences.

Lastly, there are another sort of persons, not only fit for, but necessary in plantations, and that is, men of universal spirits, that have an eye to the good of posterity, and that both understand and delight to promote good discipline and just government among a plain and well intending people; such persons may find room in colonies for their good counsel and contrivance, who are shut out from being of much use or service to great nations under settl'd customs; these men deserve much esteem, and would be hearken'd to. Doubtless 'twas this (as I observ'd before) that put some of the famous Greeks and Romans upon transplanting and regulating colonies of people in divers parts of the world; whose names, for giving so great proof of their wisdom, virtue, labour and constancy, are with justice honourably delivered down by story to the praise of our own times; though the world, after all its higher pretences of religion, barbarously errs from their excellent example.

The following selection is part of a book written by the Reverend
Hugh Jones, who came to Virginia in 1717. In it, he described,
in rather unfavorable terms, the difficulties involved in both recruiting and managing indentured servants from the British Isles.
(Source: Hugh Jones, Present State of Virginia, London, 1924,
in John R. Commons etal., ed., Documentary History of American
Industrial Society, I, Cleveland, 1910-1911.)

The ships that transport these things often call at Ireland to victual,
and bring over frequently white servkts, which are of three kinds: such as
come upon certain wages by agreement for a certain time; such as come
bound by indenture, commonly called kids, who are usually to serve four
or five years; and, those convicts or felons that are transported, whose
room they had much rather have than their company, for abundance of them
do great mischief, commit robbery and murder and spoil servants, that
were before very good. But they frequently there meet with the end that
they deserved at home, though indeed some of them prove indifferent good.
Their being sent thither to work as slaves for punishment, is but a mere
notion, for few of them ever lived so well and so easy before, especially
if they are good for anything. These are to serve seven and sometimes
fourteen years, and they and servants by indentures have an allowance
of corn and clothes, when they are out of their time, that they may be
therewith supported till they can be provided with services or otherwise
settled. With these three sorts of servants are they supplied from England,
Wales, Scotland, and Ireland, among which they that have a mind to it
may serve their time with ease and satisfaction to themselves and their
masters, especially if they fall into good hands.

These if they forsake their roguery together with the other kids . . .,
when they are free, may work day-labor, or else rent a small plantation
for a trifle almost, or else turn overseers, if they are expert, industrious
and careful, or follow their trade, if they have been brought up to any,
especially smiths, carpenters, tailors, sawyers, coopers and brick-
layers . . . The plenty of the country and the good wages given to work
folks occasion very few poor, who are supported by the parish, being
such as are lame, sick or decrepit through age, distempers, accidents, or
some infirmities. For where there is a numerous family of poor children
the vestry takes care to bind them out apprentices, till they are able to
maintain themselves by their own labor; by which means they are never
tormented with vagrant and vagabond beggars, there being a reward for
taking up runaways, that are at a small distance from their home, if they
are not known or are without a pass from their master and can give no good
account of themselves, especially Negroes.

Beginning in the 1720's, heavy Scotch-Irish emigration to America took place. The following series of letters between Hugh Boulter, the Bishop of London, and the Duke of Newcastle, explain some of the causes of this Scotch-Irish influx.
(Source: Hugh Boulter, Letters Written by His Excellency Hugh Boulter, D. D., Lord Primate of Ireland, . . ., Oxford, 1769.)

Dublin, Mar. 13, 1728

To the Bishop of London:

My Lord:---As we have had reports here that the Irish gentlemen in London would have the great burthen of tithes thought one of the chief grievances, that occasion such numbers of the people of the North going to America, I have for some time designed to write to your lordship on that subject.

But a memorial lately delivered in here by the Dissenting ministers of this place, containing the causes of this desertion, as represented to them by the letters of their brethren in the North (which memorial we have lately sent over to my lord lieutenant), mentioning the oppression of the ecclesiastical courts about tithes as one of their great grievances: I found myself under a necessity of troubling your lordship on this occasion with a true state of that affair, and of desiring your lordship to discourse with the ministry about it.

The gentlemen of this country have ever since I came hither been talking to others, and persuading their tenants, who complained of the excessiveness of their rents, that it was not the paying too much rent, but too much tithe that impoverished them: and the notion soon took among the Scotch Presbyterians, as a great part of the Protestants in the North are, who it may easily be supposed do not pay tithes with great cheerfulness. And indeed I make no doubt but the landlords in England might with great ease raise a cry amongst their tenants of the great oppression they lay under by paying tithes . . . .

What the gentlemen want to be at is, that they may go on raising their rents, and that the clergy should still receive their old payments for their tithes. But as things have happened otherwise, and they are very angry with the clergy, without considering that it could not happen otherwise than it has, since if a clergyman saw a farm raised in its rent e.g., from 10 to 20.1 per annum, he might be sure his tithe was certainly worth double what he formerly took for it. Not that I believe the clergy have made a proportionable advancement in their composition for their tithes to what the gentlemen have made in their rents. And yet it is upon this rise of the value of the tithes that they would persuade the people to throw their distress.

In a conference I had with the Dissenting ministers here some weeks ago, they mentioned the raising the value of the tithes beyond what had been formerly paid as a proof that the people were oppressed in the article of tithes. To which I told them, that the value of tithes did not prove any oppression, except it were proved that that value was greater than they were really worth, and that even then the farmer had his remedy by letting the clergy take it in kind.

And there is the less in this argument, because the fact is, that about the years 1694 and 1695, the lands here were almost wasted and unsettled, and the clergy in the last distress for tenants for their tithes, when great numbers of them were glad to let their tithes at a very low value, and that during incumbency, for few would take them on other terms: and as the country has since settled and improved, as those incumbents have dropped off, the tithe of those parties has been considerably advanced without the least oppression, but I believe your lordship will think not without some grumbling. The same, no doubt, has happened when there have been careless or needy incumbents, and others of a different character that have succeeded them.

I need not mention to your lordship that I have been forced to talk to several here, that if a landlord takes too great a portion of the profits of a farm for his share by way of rent (as the tithe will light on the tenant's share) the tenant will be impoverished: but then it is not the tithe but the increased rent that undoes the farmer. And indeed in this country, where I fear the tenant hardly ever has more than one third of the profit he makes of his farm for his share, and too often but a fourth or perhaps a fifth part, as the tenant's share is charged with the tithe, his case is no doubt hard, but it is plain from what side the hardship arises.

Another thing they complain of in their memorial is, the trouble that has been given them about their marriages and their school-masters. As to this I told them, that for some time they had not been molested about their marriages; and that as to their school-masters, I was sure they had met with very little trouble on that head, since I had never heard any such grievance so much as mentioned till I saw it in their memorial.

Another matter complained of is the sacramental test, in relation to which I told them, the laws were the same in England.

As for other grievances they mention, such as raising the rents unreasonably, the oppression of justices of the peace, seneschals, and other officers in the country, as they are by no ways of an ecclesiastical nature, I shall not trouble your lordship with an account of them, but must desire your lordship to talk with the ministry on the subject I have now wrote about, and endeavor to prevent their being prepossessed with any unjust opinion of the clergy, or being disposed, if any attempt should be made from hence to suffer us to be stript of our just rights.

Dublin, Mar. 13, 1728

To the Duke of Newcastle:

My Lord:---As we are in a very bad way here, I think myself obliged to give your Grace some account of it.

The scarcity and dearness of provision still increases in the North. Many have eaten the oats they should have sowed their land with; and except the landlords will have the good sense to furnish them with seed, a great deal of land will lye idle this year . . . .

The humour of going to America still continues, and the scarcity of provisions certainly makes many quit us.   There are now seven ships at Belfast, that are carrying off about 1000 passengers thither; and if we knew how to stop them, as most of them can neither get victuals nor work, it would be cruel to do it . . . .

The dissenting ministers here have lately delivered in a memorial, representing the grievances their brethren have assigned as the causes, in their apprehension of the great desertion in the North.   As one of these causes relates to the ecclesiastical courts here, and as it is generally repeated here that the Irish gentlemen at London are for throwing the whole occasion of this desertion on the severity of tithes, I have by this post written to the Bishop of London a very long letter on that subject, and have desired him to wait on the ministry, and discourse with them on that head.

Dublin, July 16, 1728

To the Duke of Newcastle:

My Lord:---. . . We have hundreds of families (all Protestants) removing out of the North to America; and the least obstruction in the linen manufacture, by which the North subsists, must occasion greater numbers following; and the want of silver increasing, will prove a terrible blow to that manufacture, as there will not be money to pay the poor for their small parcels of yarn.

Dublin, Nov. 23, 1728

To the Duke of Newcastle:

My Lord:---I am very sorry I am obliged to give your Grace so melancholy an account of the state of this kingdom, as I shall in this letter; but I thought it my duty to let his Majesty know our present condition in the North.   For we have had three bad harvests together there, which has made oatmeal, which is their great subsistence, much dearer than ordinary; and as our farmers here are very poor, and obliged as soon as they have their corn to sell it for ready money to pay their rents, it is much more in the power of those who have a little money, to engross corn here, and make advantage of its scarceness, than in England.

We have had for several years some agents from the colonies in America, and several masters of ships, that have gone about the country and deluded the people with stories of great plenty, and estates to be had for going for, in those parts of the world; and they have been the better able to seduce people by reason of the necessities of the poor of late.

The people that go from here make great complaints of the oppressions they suffer here, not from the Government, but from their fellow-subjects, of one kind or another, as well as of the dearness of provisions, and they say these oppressions are one reason of their going.

But whatever occasions their going, it is certain that above 4000 men, women, and children have been shipped off from hence for the West Indies [i.e., North America] within three years, and of these, above 3000 this last summer. Of these, possibly one in ten may be a man of substance, and may do well enough abroad; but the case of the rest is deplorable. The rest either hire themselves to those of substance for passage, or contract with the masters of ships for four years' servitude when they come thither; or, if they make a shift to pay for their passage, will be under the necessity of selling themselves for servants when they come there.

Georgia, the last of the British colonies to be established in America, was the dream of the English gentleman, James Ogelthorpe. He wanted to establish a utopian community for emigrating Englishmen. It is from his prospectus for his colony that this selection is excerpted.
(Source: James Ogelthorpe, Some Account of the Designs of the Trustees for Establishing the Colony of Georgia in America, London, 1733, in Peter Force, Tracts and Other Papers, I, 1836.

From the Charter. His Majesty having taken into his consideration the miserable circumstances of many of his own poor subjects, ready to perish for want, as likewise the distresses of many poor foreigners who would take refuge here from persecution, and having a princely regard to the great danger the southern frontiers of South Carolina are exposed to by reason of the small number of white inhabitants there, has out of his fatherly compassion toward his subjects been graciously pleased to grant a charter for incorporating a number of gentlemen by the name of The Trustees for establishing the Colony of Georgia in America. They are empowered to collect benefactions and lay them out in clothing, arming, sending over, and supporting colonies of the poor, whether subjects or foreigners, in Georgia. And his Majesty farther grants all his lands between the rivers Savannah and Altamaha, which he erects into a province by the name of Georgia, unto the trustees in trust for the poor and for the better support of the colony. At the desire of the gentlemen, there are clauses in the charter restraining them and their successors from receiving any salary, fee, perquisite, or profit whatsoever, by or from this undertaking, and also from receiving any grant of lands within the said district, to themselves, or in trust for them. There are farther clauses granting to the trustees proper powers for establishing and governing the colony, and liberty of conscience to all who shall settle there.

The trustees intend to relieve such unfortunate persons as cannot subsist here, and establish them in an orderly manner, so as to form a well-regulated town. As far as their fund goes, they will defray the charge of their passage to Georgia; give them necessaries, cattle, land and subsistence till such time as they can build their houses and clear some of their land. They rely for success first on the goodness of Providence, next on the compassionate disposition of the people of England; and they doubt not that much will be spared from luxury and superfluous expenses by generous tempers, when such an opportunity is offered them by the giving of 20 pounds to provide for a man or woman, or 10 pounds to a child for ever. . .

By such a colony many families who would otherwise starve will be provided for and made masters of houses and lands; the people in Great Britain to whom these necessitous families were a burden will be relieved; numbers of manufacturers will be here employed for supplying them with clothes, working tools, and other necessaries, and by giving refuge to the distressed Salzburgers, and other persecuted Protestants, the power of

Britain, as a reward for its hospitality, will be increased by the addition of so many religious and industrious subjects.

The colony of Georgia lying about the same latitude with part of China, Persia, Palestine, and the Madeiras, it is highly probable that when hereafter it shall be well peopled and rightly cultivated, England may be supplied from thence with raw silk, wine, oil, dyes, drugs, and many other materials for manufactures which she is obliged to purchase from southern countries. As towns are established and grow populous along the rivers Savannah and Altamaha, they will make such a barrier as will render the southern frontier of the British colonies on the continent of America safe from Indian and other enemies.

All human affairs are so subject to chance that there is no answering for events; yet from reason and the nature of things it may be concluded that the riches and also the number of the inhabitants in Great Britain will be increased by importing at a cheap rate from this new colony, the materials requisite for carrying on in Britain several manufacturers will be encouraged to marry and multiply when they find themselves in circumstances to provide for their families, which must necessarily be the happy effect of the increase and cheapness of our materials of those manufactures which at present we purchase with our money from foreign countries at dear rates; and also many people will find employment here on account of such farther demands by the people of this colony for those manufactures which are made for the produce of our own country, and, as has been justly observed, the people will always abound where there is full employment for them.

Christianity will be extended by the execution of this design, since the good discipline established by the society will reform the manners of those miserable objects who shall be by them subsisted, and the example of a whole colony, who shall behave in a just, moral, and religious manner, will contribute greatly towards the conversion of the Indians, and taking off the prejudices received from the profligate lives of such who have scarce anything of Christianity but the name.

The trustees in their general meetings will consider of the most prudent methods for effectually establishing a regular colony, and that it may be done is demonstrable. Under what difficulties was Virginia planted? The coast and climate then unknown, the Indians numerous and at enmity with the first planters, who were forced to fetch all provisions from England; yet it is grown a mighty province and the revenue receives 100,000 pounds for duties upon the goods that they send yearly home. Within this fifty years by the wise economy of William Penn and those who assisted him, it now gives food to eighty thousand inhabitants and can boast of as fine a city as most in Europe.

This new colony is more likely to succeed than either of the former were, since Carolina abounds with provisions, the climate is known, and there are men to instruct in the seasons and nature of cultivating the soil. There are but few Indian families within four hundred miles, and those in perfect amity with the English. Port Royal (the station of his Majesty's ships) is within thirty, and Charleston (a great mart) is within 120 miles. If the colony is attacked it may be relieved by sea from Port Royal or the Bahamas, and the militia of South Carolina is ready to support it by land. . .

The lot of the British indentured servant in America was not always a contented one. What follows are some advertisements that appeared in colonial newspapers concerning runaway English and Welsh servants.
(Source: Virginia Gazette, South Carolina Gazette, in John R. Commons etal, eds., Documentary History . . . ., I, Cleveland, 1910-1911.)

Ran away some time in June last, from William Pierce of Nansemond County, near Mr. Theophilus Pugh's, merchant, a convict servant woman named Winifred Thomas. She is Welsh woman, short, black-haired and young; marked on the inside of her right arm with gunpowder, W. T., and the date of the year underneath. She knits and spins, and is supposed to be gone into North Carolina by the way of Cureatuck and Roanoke Inlet. Whoever brings her to her master shall be paid a pistole besides what the law allows, paid by

William Pierce.

Run away on the fifth instant from Robert Williams' plantation in Georgia, three men servants. One named James Powell, is a bricklayer by trade. About five feet nine inches high, a strong made man, born in Wiltshire, talks broad; and when he went away he wore his own short hair, with a white cap. Among his comrades he was called Alderman.

Another, named Charles Gastril, did formerly belong to the pilot boat at Pill, near Bristol; is by trade a sawyer. He is about 5 feet 10 inches high, of a thin, spare make, raw boned, and has a scar somewhere on his upper lip; aged about 25.

The third, named Jenkin James, a lusty young fellow, about the same height as Gastril, had a good fresh complexion. Bred by trade a tailor, but of late has been used to sawing, talks very much Welshly, and had on when he went away a coarse red coat and waistcoat, the buttons and buttonholes of the coat black.

Any person or persons who apprehend them, or either of them, and bring them to Mr. Thomas Jenys in Charleston, or to the said Mr. Robert Williams in Savannah shall receive 10 currency of South Carolina for each.

Robert Williams

Besides the above mentioned reward, there is a considerable sum allowed by the trustees of the colony of Georgia for taking run away servants.

N. B. About a fortnight ago, three other of the said Robert Williams' servants run away, who are already advertised.

Various methods for stimulating emigration from England to America were used. Very often, they took the form of concerted promotional efforts, frequently misrepresenting the real opportunities that existed. What follows is a description of these tactics.

(Source: William Eddis, Letters From America, Historical and Descriptive; Comprising Occurrences from 1769 to 1777, Inclusive, London, 1792.

In your frequent excursions about the great metropolis, you cannot but observe numerous advertisements, offering the most seducing encouragement to adventurers under every possible description; to those who are disgusted with the frowns of fortune in their native land, and to those of an enterprising disposition who are tempted to court her smiles in a distant region. These persons are referred to agents, or crimps, who represent the advantages to be obtained in America, in colours so alluring that it is almost impossible to resist their artifices. Unwary persons are accordingly induced to enter into articles by which they engage to become servants, agreeable to their respective qualifications, for the term of five years, every necessary accommodation being found them during the voyage, and every method taken that they may be treated with tenderness and humanity during the period of servitude, at the expiration of which they are taught to expect that opportunities will assuredly offer to secure to the honest and industrious a competent provision for the remainder of their days.

The generality of the inhabitants in this province Maryland are very little acquainted with those fallacious pretences, by which numbers are continually induced to embark for this continent. On the contrary, they too generally conceive an opinion that the difference is merely nominal between the indented servant and the convicted felon; nor will they readily believe that people who had the least experience in life, and whose characters were unexceptionable, would abandon their friends and families, and their ancient connections, for a servile situation in a remote appendage to the British Empire. From this persuasion they rather consider the convict as the more profitable servant, his term being for seven, the latter only for five years: and I am sorry to observe that there are but few instances wherein they experience different treatment . . . .

Shortly before the issuance of the Declaration of Independence, a county convention in Pennsylvania, comprised primarily of Scotch-Irish settlers, drew up a series of resolutions, which can be said to mark the beginning of official declarations of American independence.

(Source: Henry J. Ford, The Scotch-Irish in America, New York, 1915.)

Charlotte-Town, Mecklenburg County, May 31,1775.

This day the Committee of this county met, and passed the following Resolves:

WHEREAS by an Address presented to his Majesty by both Houses of Parliament, in February last, the American colonies are declared to be in a state of actual rebellion, we conceive, that all laws and commissions confirmed by, or derived from the authority of the King or Parliament, are annulled and vacated, and the former civil constitution of these colonies, for the present, wholly suspended. To provide, in some degree, for the exigencies of this country, in the present alarming period, we deem it proper and necessary to pass the following Resolves, viz.

I---That all commissions, civil and military, heretofore granted by the Crown, to be exercised in these colonies, are null and void, and the constitution of each particular colony wholly suspended.

II--That the Provincial Congress of each province, under the direction of the great Continental Congress, is invested with all legislative and executive powers within their respective provinces; and that no other legislative or executive power, does, or can exist, at this time, in any of these colonies.

III--As all former laws are now suspended in this province, and the Congress have not yet provided others, we judge it necessary, for better preservation of good order, to form certain rules and regulations for the internal government of this county, until laws shall be provided for us by the Congress.

IV--That the inhabitants of this county do meet on a certain day appointed by this Committee, and having formed themselves into nine companies, (to wit) eight in the county, and one in the town of Charlotte, do chuse a Colonel and other military officers, who shall hold and exercise their several powers by virtue of this choice, and independent of the Crown of Great-Britain, and former constitution of this province.

V--That for the better preservation of the peace and administration of justice, each of those companies do chuse from their own body, two discreet freeholders, who shall be empowered, each by himself and singly, to decide and determine all matters of controversy, arising within said company, under the sum of twenty shillings; and jointly and together, all controversies under the sum of forty shillings; yet so as that their decisions may admit of appeal to the Convention of the Select-Men of the county; and also that any one of these men, shall have power to examine and commit to confinement persons accused of petit larceny.

119

VI--That those two Select-Men, thus chosen, do jointly and together chuse from the body of their particular company, two persons properly qualified to act as Constables, who may assist them in the execution of their offiee.

VII--That upon the complaint of any persons to either of these Select-Men, he do issue his warrant, directed to the Constable, commanding him to bring the aggressor before him or them, to answer said complaint.

VIII--That these eighteen Select-Men, thus appointed, do meet every third Thursday in January, April, July, and October, at the Court-House, in Charlotte, to hear and determine all matters of controversy, for sums exceeding forty shillings, also appeals; and in cases of felony, to commit the person or persons convicted thereof to close confinement, until the Provincial Congress shall provide and establish laws and modes of proceeding in all such cases.

IX--That these eighteen Select-Men, thus convened, do chuse a Clerk, to record the transactions of said Convention, and that said clerk, upon the application of any person or persons aggrieved, do issue his warrant to one of the Constables of the company to which the offender belongs, directing said Constable to summons and warn said offender to appear before the Convention, at their next sitting, to answer the aforesaid complaint.

X--That any person making complaint upon oath, to the Clerk, or any member of the Convention, that he has reason to suspect, that any person or persons indebted to him, in a sum above forty shillings, intend clandestinely to withdraw from the county, without paying such debt, the Clerk or such member shall issue his warrant to the Constable, commanding him to take said person or persons into safe custody, until the next sitting of the Convention.

XI--That when a debtor for a sum below forty shillings shall abscond and leave the county, the warrant granted as aforesaid, shall extend to any goods or chattels of said debtor, as may be found, and such goods or chattels beseized and held in custody by the Constable, for the space of thirty days; in which time, if the debtor fail to return and discharge the debt, the Constable shall return the warrant to one of the Select-Men of the company, where the goods are found, who, shall issue orders to the Constable to sell such a part of said goods, as shall amount to the sum due: That when the debt exceeds forty shillings, the return shall be made to the Convention, who shall issue orders for sale.

XII--That all receivers and collectors of quit-rents, public and county taxes, do pay the same into the hands of the chairman of this Committee, to be by them disbursed as the public exigencies may require; and such receivers and collectors proceed no further in their office, until they be approved of by, and have given to, this Committee, good and sufficient security, for a faithful return of such monies when collected.

XIII--That the Committee be accountable to the county for the application of all monies received from such public officers.

XIV--That all these officers hold their commissions during the pleasure of their several constituents.

XV--That this Committee will sustain all damages that ever hereafter may accrue to all or any of these officers thus appointed, and thus acting on account of their obedience and conformity to these Resolves.

XVI--That whatever person shall hereafter receive a commission from the Crown, or attempt to exercise any such commission heretofore received, shall be deemed an enemy to his country, and upon information being made to the Captain of the company in which he resides, the said company shall cause him to be apprehended, and conveyed before two Select-Men of the said company, who upon proof of the fact, shall commit him, the said offender, to safe custody, until the next sitting of the Committee, who shall deal with him as prudence may direct.

XVII--That any person refusing to yield obedience to the above Resolves, shall be considered equally criminal, and liable to the same punishment, as the offenders above last mentioned.

XVIII--That these Resolves be in full force and virtue, until instructions from the Provincial Congress, regulating the jurisprudence of the province, shall provide otherwise, or the legislative body of Great-Britain, resign its unjust and arbitrary pretentions with respect to America.

XIX--That the eight militia companies in the county, provide themselves with proper arms and accoutrements, and hold themselves in readiness to execute the commands and directions of the General Congress of this province and this Committee.

XX--That the Committee appoint Colonel Thomas Polk, and Doctor Joseph Kenedy, to purchase 300 lb. of powder, 600 lb. of lead, 1000 flints, for the use of the militia of this county, and deposit the same in such place as the Committee may hereafter direct.

Signed by order of the Committee,

EPH. BREVARD, Clerk of the Committee.

The English reformer, Morris Birkbeck, came to America with the intention of founding a settlement for English immigrants in the prospective state of Illinois. Along with his friend, George Flower, he established the community in 1817-1818. This is part of an account of that settlement.

(Source: George Flower, History of the English Settlement in Edwards County, Illinois, founded in 1817 and 1818 by Morris Birkbeck and George Flower, with preface and footnotes by E. B. Washburne, in Chicago Historical Society, Collections, I, 1882.)

In about three years [after the original foundation of the settlement] , a surplus of corn, pork, and beef was obtained, but no market. Before they could derive any benefit from the sale of their surplus produce, the farmers themselves had to quit their farms and open the channels of commerce, and convey their produce along until they found a market. At first there were no produce-buyers, and the first attempts at mercantile adventures were almost failures. In the rising towns, a few buyers began to appear, but with too small a capital to pay money, even at the low price produce then was. They generally bought on credit, to pay on their return from New Orleans. In this way, the farmers were at disadvantage; if the markets were good, the merchant made a handsome profit. If bad, they often had not enough to pay the farmer. Then the farmers began to build their own flat-boats, load them with the produce of their own growth, and navigate them by their own hands. They traded down the Mississippi to New Orleans, and often on the coast beyond. Thus were the channels of trade opened, and in this way was the chief trade of the country carried on for many years . . . .

One evening . . . we discussed the measures that should be taken to form some village or town, as a centre for those useful arts necessary to agriculture. Every person wanted the services of a carpenter and blacksmith. But every farmer could not build workshops at his own door . . . . Thus the spot for our town as a central situation was decided upon. Now for a name . . . . At last we did what almost all emigrants do, patched on a name that had its association with the land of our birth. Albion was then and there located, built, and peopled in imagination . . . .

We met the next day in the woods according to appointment. The spot seemed suitable . . . . "Here shall be the centre of our town," we said . . . . Mr. Fordham . . . forthwith went to work, and completed the survey and the plat. One of our number went to Shawneetown, and entered the section of six hundred and forty acres, which was laid off in town lots. The public square was in the middle . . . .

The first double-cabin built, was designated for a tavern, and a single one for its stable . . . . Another and second double and single cabin were occupied as dwelling and shop by a blacksmith. I had brought bellows, anvils, tools, and appliances for three or four blacksmith-shops, from the City of Birmingham, England. There were three brothers that came with Mr. Charles Trimmer, all excellent mechanics.

122

. . . Jacob, the blacksmith, was immediately installed, and went to work. There stood Albion, no longer a myth, but a reality, a fixed fact. A log-tavern and a blacksmith-shop.

Two germs of civilization were now planted---one of the useful arts, the other a necessary institution of present civilization. Any man could now get his horse shod and get drunk in Albion, privileges which were soon enjoyed, the latter especially . . . .

The town-proprietors, at first four, afterwards increased to eight (each share five hundred dollars), went to work vigorously. They put up cabin after cabin, which were occupied as soon as put up, by emigrants coming in. The builders of these were the backwoodsmen, some from twenty to thirty miles distant. Attracted by our good money and good whiskey, these new gathered in . . . .

The publication in England of our travels, my return, and personal communication with a host of individuals, had given a wide-spread knowledge of what we had done and what we intended to do. Our call had received a response from the farmers of England, the miners of Cornwall, the drovers of Wales, the mechanics of Scotland, the West-India planter, the inhabitants of the Channel Isles, and the "gentleman of no particular business" of the Emerald Isle. All were moving or preparing to move to join us in another hemisphere. The cockneys of London had decided on the reversal of their city habits, to breathe the fresh air of the prairies. Parties were moving, or preparing to move, in all directions. . . .

The Lawrence-and-Trimmer party [which sailed from Bristol] landed safely at Philadelphia early in June [1819] . They made their way some in wagons some on horseback, over the mountains to Pittsburgh, then descending the Ohio in flatboats to Shawneetown, in August, proceeded without delay on foot, in wagons and on horseback, to Mr. Birkbeck's cabin on Boltenhouse Prairie . . . .

It is a noticeable fact that emigrants bound for the English Settlement in Illinois, landed at every port from the St. Lawrence to the Gulf of Mexico. This arises from the fact that the laborers and small-farmers of England are very imperfectly acquainted with the geography of America. Indeed, among all classes in England there is a very inadequate idea of the extent of the United States . . . . As various as their ports of debarkation, were the routes they took, and the modes of conveyance they adopted.

Some came in wagons and light carriages, overland; some on horseback; some in arks; some in skiffs; and some by steamboat, by New Orleans. One Welshman landed at Charleston, S. C. "How did you get here?" I asked. "Oh," he innocently replied, "I just bought me a horse, sir, and inquired the way." It seems our Settlement was then known at the plantations in Carolina and in the mountains of Tennessee. The great variety found among our people, coming as they did from almost every county in the kingdom, in complexion, stature, and dialect, was in the early days of our Settlement very remarkable . . . .

Individuals and families were frequently arriving, and occasionally a party of thirty and forty. A fresh cause induced this tide of emigration. It arose from the private correspondence of the first poor men who came. Having done well themselves, and by a few years of hard labor acquired.

more wealth than they ever expected to obtain they wrote home to friend
or relative an account of their success. These letters handed round
in the remote villages of England, in which many of them lived, reached
individuals in a class to whom information in book form was wholly in-
accessible. Each letter had its scores of readers, and, passing from hand
to hand, traversed its scores of miles. The writer, known at home as a
poor man, earning perhaps a scanty subsistence by his daily labor, telling
of the wages he received, his bountiful living, of his own farm and the number of his live-stock, produced a greater impression in the limited circle
of its readers than a printed publication had the power of doing. His fellow-
laborer who heard these accounts, and feeling that he was no better off
than when his fellow-laborer left him for America, now exerted every nerve
to come and do likewise . . . .

Emigrant guide books were always quite popular with prospective settlers. What follows is an excerpt from one written by John Knight, and published in England, which told of the associative effort new immigrants would find on the American frontier. (Source: John Knight, <u>The Emigrants Best Instructor, or, The Most Recent and Important Information Respecting the United States of America, Selected From the Works of the Latest Travellers in that Country,</u> Manchester, 1818.)

. . . In the settlement of a country, there are many things to be done, which require the united strength of many; this money cannot purchase: but that kind and generous feeling, which men (not rendered callous by wealth or poverty) have for each other, comes to their relief. The neighbors, (even unsolicited) appoint a day, when as a frolic, they shall (for instance,) build the new settler a house.---On the morning appointed, they assemble; and divide themselves into parties: one party cut down the trees; another lops them and cuts them into proper lengths; a third, (with horses or oxen) drag them to the intended spot; another party make shingles for the roof; and at night all the materials are on the spot: - and the night of the next day, the family sleep in their new habitation.---No payment is expected, nor would be received: it is considered a duty; and lays him under obligation, to assist the next settler. But this cooperation of labour is not confined to new settlers; it occurs frequently, in the course of a year, amongst the old settlers with whom it is a bond of amity and social intercourse: and in no part of the world, is good neighbourship, in greater perfection, than in America.

The British government enacted a series of new regulations concerning emigration. By 1835, it was the general concensus that these new acts had failed to stop all of the evils attendent to British emigration. In this selection, a British economist discussed the failure of these policies.

(Source: John Ramsay McCulloch, A Dictionary, Practical, Theoretical, and Historical, of Commerce and Commercial Navigation, I, Philadelphia, 1847.)

. . . . During 1833, 1834, and 1835, no fewer than 183,237 voluntary emigrants left the United Kingdom; 173,344 being destined for America, and 9,893 for the Australian colonies and the Cape of Good Hope. Such being the extent to which emigration is carried, the propriety, or rather necessity, of enacting some general regulations, with respect to the conveyance of emigrants to their destination, must be obvious to every one at all acquainted with the subject. The great number of emigrants are in humble life; few among them know anything of ships, or of the precautions necessary to insure a safe and comfortable voyage; they are, also, for the most part poor, and exceedingly anxious to economise, so that they seldom hesitate to embark in any ship, however unfit for the conveyance of passengers, or inadequately supplied with provisions, provided it be cheap. Unprincipled masters and owners have not been slow to take advantage of this, and in order to prevent the frauds that have been, and that would be, practised on the unwary, it has been found indispensable to lay down some general regulations as to the number of passengers to be taken on board ships as compared with their tonnage, the quantity of water and provisions as compared with the passengers, etc. But this is no very easy task. If the limitations be too strict, that is, if comparatively few passengers may be carried, or if the stock of provisions to be put on board be either unnecessarily large or expensive, the cost of emigration is proportionally enhanced; and an artificial and serious impediment is thrown in the way of what ought to be made as easy as possible, consistent with security. But, on the other hand, if too many passengers be allowed, their health is liable to suffer; and should the supply of provisions be inadequate, or the quality bad, the most serious consequences may ensue. The Passage Act (6 G. 4. c. 116) obliged too great a quantity of expensive provisions to be put on board, and was, in consequence, objected to by emigrants as well as shippers. The act 9 G. 4. c. 21 (1828) avoided this error; but it, too, was defective, inasmuch as it made no provision with respect to the sufficiency of the ship, the having a surgeon or other properly qualified medical person on board ships carrying a certain number of passengers, and in other particulars.

These deficiencies have been in part supplied by the act of 1835 (5 and 6 W. 4. c. 53) . . . . . But we doubt whether even it will completely answer the end in view. During 1834 no fewer than 17 ships, with passengers on board, bound for Quebec, were wrecked on the passage; 731 emigrants losing their lives in consequence, while many more lost most part of their property, and were reduced to the greatest difficulties. These losses principally took place in the gulf and river of St. Lawrence; but we should err if we ascribed them entirely, or principally even, to the difficulty of the navigation. Emigrants to Quebec are mostly taken out in ship; engaged in the timber trade; and it is well known that, speaking generally, these are a very inferior class; it being the usual practice to turn worn out ships, unfit to carry dry cargoes, into this department. Most part of the catastrophes alluded to may, we are assured, be ascribed to this circumstance, and to the misconduct of the masters and crews. We doubt whether the clause in the present act as to the seaworthiness of the ship will be sufficient to obviate the disasters arising from the use of improper vessels . . . . .There can be no question as to its being the bounden duty of government to take every reasonable precaution for obviating shipwreck. And, even if higher considerations did not make an effectual interference imperative, it is pretty certain that the check given to emigration to Canada, by the shipwrecks and destruction of life that have recently taken place, is much greater than any that could be given by the trifling addition that the adoption of some such plan as has now been suggested would make to its cost . . . .

The new act does not make it imperative on ships conveying passengers to America to have a surgeon on board; and, perhaps, when bound for New York, he may not be required. But the voyage to Quebec is often very tedious; and much suffering and loss of life have frequently arisen from no medical officer being on board emigrant ships destined for that port.

It has been said, that if we lay constrictions on the conveyance of emigrants to Quebec, it will make New York the great landing port, and throw the business of their conveyance entirely into the hands of the Americans. But the regulations enforced in the subjoined act, and those we have suggested, apply equally to both parties. And it is, besides, true that a continuance of the old system, attended as it, no doubt, would have been by a repetition of the most appalling disasters, would have had the very effect falsely ascribed to judicious regulations. It would have prevented anyone not compelled by necessity---who was not, in fact, a beggar---from sailing in a vessel bound for Quebec.

A constant complaint coming from native Americans was that the British government was allowing, if not encouraging the emigration of hordes of their pauperized and undersireable subjects. Reports of American consular officials stationed in various British cities seem to agree with this opinion.
(Source: "Report from the Secretary of the Treasury, Relative to the Deportation of Paupers from Great Britain, etc., in Obedience to the Resolution of the Senate of the 4th of July, 1836," U. S. 24th Congress, 2nd Session, Senate Document, No. 5.)

From the United States Consulate at Londonderry
(letter of September 19, 1836):

. . . . There has been for many years past, and still continues, a large emigration from this port to different parts of the United States, and also to the British settlements in North America; and, from my knowledge on the subject, I have no hesitation in stating that the description of persons who generally embark for the United States from this port are of good character, in comfortable circumstances, and certainly many degrees removed from paupers.

On the contrary, the greater number of the persons who embark for the British settlements, on account of the cheap conveyance, are the evil and ill-disposed, who will not do well in their own country, and the landed proprietors are glad to get rid of them, which they do by paying their passages, and laying in sufficient provisions for the voyage, totally regardless of how they are to make out life on their arrival.

The reason why North America is preferred is on account of the cheapness of the passage . . . . .

From the United States Consulate at Liverpool
(letter of September 15, 1836):

. . . . I find it has been the practice with many parishes, for some years past, to send abroad such of their superabundant population as would consent to go, and although there has never been a restriction as to the place, they have invariably preferred the United States, and ninety out of a hundred, New York. Regular contracts are made by the different parishes with passenger-brokers at this place to ship them; the extent of this deportation, however, always limited in comparison with the general emigration, has recently been much diminished, in consequence, probably, of the increased demand for labor and the general prosperity of the country. The following facts are obtained from authentic sources and may be relied on. In all instances the emigration is voluntary, and the parish is not relieved by it from its obligation of support should the individual ever return. Convicts are never sent, nor the inmates of work-houses, nor those who, from age or decrepitude, are unable to support themselves. Not one person out of fifty is over fifty years old; they are generally young people who have made improvident marriages, and, without ostensible means of support, with increasing families are likely to become chargeable to their parish. Reputed poachers are a class of people frequently sent from agricultural districts, and out of at least a thousand, of various descriptions, shipped off by one of my informants, he is quite sure not more that twenty have ever returned. Some provision is always made for their immediate support, on landing at their place of destination. From five to ten pounds is paid by the shipping agent to each individual on the vessel's leaving port, besides their passages being paid for, and their provisions found for the voyage.

In the year 1830, the emigration from this port to the United States is estimated at sixteen thousand; out of which about six hundred were sent by different parishes. In 1832 there were about five hundred sent at parish expense; since when, not more than three hundred have gone in a similar way in any one year; and during the last, although the general emigration was greater than at any former period, out of twenty-four or twenty-five thousand there were but about one hundred and fifty paupers . . . . .

From United States Consulate Kingston-upon-Hull
(letter of August 30, 1836):

. . . . No list that can be relied on, of passengers sailing from Hull, is kept at the custom-house, which distinguishes the paupers from those of a better class; regular muster-rolls are kept, but the parties are merely described by their names, ages, and from whence they come and occupation.

The officers of the customs are well aware that paupers do proceed, both to the United States and Canada, and it has been admitted by the owners of several vessels sailing there, that their passages are paid by the overseers of the parishes to which they belong. The mode of doing this varies according to the trustworthiness of the pauper; if good, he is trusted to make his own bargain, and generally has a trifle of money advanced to him for use when he quits the vessel, to enable him to get up the country. If the man is a bad character, he is generally the best off, as the overseers pay his passage-money and procure for him the necessaries for his voyage. The man then turns restive, and oftentimes refuses to go unless more money is given him, generally 5 or 10 more than was first agreed on. So that the worse the character the better able the pauper is to make his way when he quits the vessel.

As thousands of British immigrants flocked to American shores during the 1830's, a large percentage of them found employment in the textile mills of Lowell and Waltham, Massachusetts. This selection is a description of the conditions under which these immigrants, especially the Scotch and English, labored; and most of all about the immigrant girls in these factories.
(Source: Harriet Martineau, Society in America, I, London, 1837.)

I visited the corporate factory establishment at Waltham, within a few miles of Boston. The Waltham Mills were at work before those of Lowell were set up. The establishment is for the spinning and weaving of cotton alone, and the construction of the requisite machinery. Five hundred persons were employed at the time of my visit. The girls earn two, and some three, dollars a week, besides their board. The little children earn one dollar a week. Most of the girls live in the houses provided by the corporation, which accommodate from six to eight each. When sisters come to the mill, it is a common practice for them to bring their mother to keep house for them and some of their companions, in a dwelling built by their own earnings. In this case, they save enough out of their own board to clothe themselves, and have their two or three dollars a week to spare. Some have thus cleared off mortgages from their fathers' farms; others have educated the hope of the family at college; and many are rapidly accumulating an independence. I saw a whole street of houses built with the earnings of the girls; some with piazzas, and green venetian blinds; and all neat and sufficiently spacious.

The factory people built the church, which stands conspicuous on the green in the midst of the place. The minister's salary (eight hundred dollars last year) is raised by a tax on the pews. The corporation gave them a building for a lyceum, which they have furnished with a good library, and where they have lectures every winter . . . .

The managers of the various factory establishments keep the wages as nearly equal as possible, and then let the girls freely shift about from one to another. When a girl comes to the overseer to inform him of her intention of working at the mill, he welcomes her, and asks how long she means to stay. It may be six months, or a year, or five years, or for life. She declares what she considers herself fit for, and sets to work accordingly. If she finds that she cannot work so as to keep up with the companion appointed to her, or to please her employer or herself, she comes to the overseer, and volunteers to pick cotton, or sweep the rooms, or undertake some other service that she can perform.

The people work about seventy hours per week, on the average. The amount of work varies with the length of the days, the wages continuing the same. All look like well-dressed young ladies. The health is good; or rather (as this is too much to be said about health anywhere in the United States), it is no worse than it is elsewhere . . . .

The shoemaking at Lynn is carried on almost entirely in private dwellings from the circumstance that the people who do it are almost all farmers or fishermen likewise. A stranger who has not been enlightened upon the ways of the place would be astonished at the number of small square erections, like miniature schoolhouses, standing each as an appendage to a dwelling-house. These are the "shoe shops," where the father of the family and his boys work, while the women within are employed in binding and trimming. Thirty or more of these shoe shops may be counted in a walk of half-a-mile. When a Lynn shoe manufacturer receives an order, he issues the tidings. The leather is cut out by men on his premises; and then the work is given to those who apply for it; if possible, in small quantities, for the sake of dispatch. The shoes are brought home on Friday night, packed off on Saturday, and in a fortnight or three weeks are on the feet of dwellers in all parts of the Union. The whole family works upon shoes during the winter; and in the summer, the father and sons turn out into the fields, or go fishing. I knew of an instance where a little boy and girl maintained the whole family, while the earnings of the rest went to build a house. I saw very few shabby houses . . . . The place is unboundedly prosperous, through the temperance and industry of the people. The deposits in the Lynn Savings' Bank in 1834, were about $34,000, the population of the town being then four thousand. Since that time, both the population and the prosperity have much increased. It must be remembered, too, that the mechanics of America have more uses for their money than are open to the operatives of England. They build houses, buy land, and educate their sons and daughters.

Although the Federal government investigated the problem of British paupers coming to the United States, it was left to the individual states to deal with the question. This selection, an extract from a report of a Massachusetts House of Representatives committee, discussed the burden of British pauperism in their state.
(Source: Report of a Committee of the Massachusetts House of Representatives, on "The Introduction into the United States of Paupers From Foreign Countries, April 18, 1836," in U. S. 24th Congress, 1st Session, House Document, No. 219.)

Commonwealth of Massachusetts, House of Representatives
April 9, 1836

The Committee appointed by this House, on the 25th ultimo, "to consider the expediency of instructing the Senators and requesting the Representatives of this Commonwealth in the Congress of the United States, to use their endeavors to obtain the passage of a law by Congress to prevent the introduction of foreign paupers into this country, or to favor any other measures which Congress may be disposed to adopt to effect the object," have attended to the duty assigned them, and respectfully ask leave to report:

That, at this late period in the session of this Legislature, they have not thought it advisable to go into the minute details of this most interesting, not to say alarming, subject, especially as it has occupied so much of the attention of this House for several of the last years, and so much valuable information relating to it has heretofore been communicated. They have preferred to come directly to the point referred to their consideration, adverting only so such circumstances as seemed to have a direct bearing upon it.

The immense, insupportable, and by us almost inconceivable, burden of pauperism in England, which originated at first in a well intended but ill judged and most disastrous provision of law, would most naturally occupy the attention of her statesmen and philanthropists, and induce them to look in every direction for some efficient mode of relief. And it is not at all surprising that the peculiar facilities and inducements for the emigration of paupers to this country, in our immediate contiguity to the British provinces, in our extended seacoast, and more than all perhaps, in the comfortable provision here made for the poor, and "our open philanthropy and freedom in giving strangers a hearty welcome to our shores," have decided them to fix upon emigration hither as the most available measure. Former

132

Committees of this House have perceived and pointed out the gradual developments of a plan to this effect. They have also perceived the insufficiency of any State enactments "effectually" to prevent the rapid ingress of paupers to this country, under the operations of such a plan. An appeal to Congress has been considered the only adequate remedy of the evil. But, so far as your Committee have been informed, no such appeal has yet been made. They are solemnly of the opinion, however, that it cannot safely be any longer delayed. They have ascertained that the plan of His Majesty's poor law commissioners, recommending the emigration of their poor, has not only reached its maturity in positive enactments of law, but has actually gone into operation . . . . .

Your committee find that . . . . . 320 paupers, from nineteen parishes, in eleven different counties, are reported to have emigrated during the last year. Of these 320, the cost of whose transportation was 2,473, or about £ 7,15s.6d. per head, 9 went to Prince Edward's Island, 261 to Upper Canada, and the remaining 50 to the United States, notwithstanding the regulation restricting them "to some British colony."

Now let it be considered that England contains 15,635 parishes and that if they should all conclude, this year to follow the example of the 19 reported, so "signally beneficial" in its results, our proportion of them would be about 41,145. But, alarming as this simple calculation may seem, it is but a trifle to what we have every reason to fear. When we consider that these paupers have no claim whatever upon the provinces to the United States; and the fact, so many times communicated to this Legislature, that nearly all of the host of foreign paupers, with which we are already infested, have come in by land through the provinces; is there not reason enough to fear that we shall soon be inundated with population of this kind, if it cannot, by some means, be speedily prevented? - No comment, surely, is necessary upon the fact that 261 of the 320 above-mentioned emigrants came to Upper Canada. Can it be for a moment supposed that England intends thus to burden her colonies, or that her colonies will quietly receive and provide for such accessions to their population?

As the result of their inquiries, therefore, your committee will only add the appended resolve . . . . .

Resolved, That it is expedient to instruct the Senators and request the Representatives of this Commonwealth, in the Congress of the United States, to use their endeavors to obtain the passage of a law by Congress to prevent the introduction of foreign paupers into this country; or to favor any other measures which Congress may be disposed to adopt to effect the object.

As with other immigrant groups, the British formed their own clubs and societies, which helped to protect the newcomers from fraud, and which helped them to adjust to American life. This excerpt is a portion of a report delivered before a committee of the New York State Assembly by the secretary of one of these societies.

(Source: New York State Assembly Document, No. 60, 46, 1846.)

William L. Roy, of the city of Brooklyn being duly sworn, deposes and says, that he is over forty-five years of age, that he has been secretary of the United States Immigrant Society for the protection of English and Scotch immigrants, for the last three years. That these societies were formed principally to protect the English or Scotch immigrants from the frauds practiced upon them on their arrival in this country. That the resident English and Scotch were made conversant with so many evils and frauds committed upon their countrymen that they deemed it an act of humanity to protect them on their arrival; and in saving their own countrymen from these evils, they ascertained that other immigrants also suffered from similar causes, and their efforts have also been directed to relieve the Irishman, German, and indeed, all who sought the free institutions and liberal views of this country, and a freedom from the oppressions of the old world; and for similar purposes, other societies have been formed in the city, and all done more or less for the relief of the ignorant and oppressed, the sick and the poor, as they come to our shores. This examination has enabled the benevolent to discover evils incident to the present quarantine laws, and the citizens who have associated themselves for the benevolent purpose of aiding their friends or strangers find that the law is now, in many respects, oppressive, and might be remedied with safety to the health of the city, and at the same time add to the happiness of many objects of humanity, and keep the stranger from the ills incident to the operation of the law as it now exists. The property of these individuals is often unjustly taken, their morals injured, their health destroyed, and they not unfrequently prevented from becoming good citizens by being driven from the correct channels of citizenship, to the waywardness and crime of dissipation, poverty and despair.

That on arrival of vessels from Europe with steerage passengers, during the summer months, they are required to remain at quarantine, land their passengers, and they be brought to the city by lighters. That this subjects the immigrants to be sent to the quarantine dock immediately, and the bunks for the sleeping of the passengers are immediately broken up, and the passengers to be taken from the dock in open and uncovered lighters to the city or interior. That in the crowding of great numbers at a time, and the necessity of having their baggage examined in great haste, often baggage is lost, the passengers out without a shade in a hot sun for a long time, or exposed to the night air, rains and storms, without any comfortable places

134

for rest, and without food; and landed at a wharf in a strange city, at all hours, which creates the necessity of engaging lodgings without any judgment, or passages west, and paying for them without knowing to whom the money is going, or whether they will be justly credited therewith, or if credited with what is paid; whether the price paid is not exorbitant. These ills, necessary to a just performance of duty, are very great; but when enhanced by those which the cupidity of man devises, they become so severe that Heaven calls for relief.

Persons are allowed to go on shipboard, the lighters, and on the wharves in the city, who make representations which prove to be false; lead the immigrant into houses in the city unfit for man to live in and they require exorbitant pay' or take money for the transporting of the immigrant west, and give worthless tickets for a passage, or charge a very much larger price than the actual charge by respectable and responsible lines of steam or canal boats. Cases, which come under the evils above enumerated, are very frequent and very grievous, and the fact that some vessels arrive with from three to five hundred passengers each, and together bring to our port from 60,000 to 80,000 immigrants annually, and they principally in the summer months, make the evils not only great in individual cases, but enormous when looked at in the aggregate.

B.   A Legislative Committee's Report

. . . . The reports and rumors which have, from time to time, appeared in the public newspapers, within the last year, of the frauds and impositions practiced upon these strangers in our land, have fallen vastly short of the reality. It . . . . appears that this is no new invention, but that these frauds have been carried on for several years to a more limited extent, without attracting much notice, or seeming to excite much interest among those who should be the first to protect and the last to prey upon this class of their fellow beings. But it has been left to the present year, when the increase of emigration, owing to causes well known to exist in the old world, has been not only beyond all former precedent, but beyond all calculation, for those who make it their business to subsist by defrauding and plundering these people, to realize a golden harvest.

Your committee must confess, that they had no conception of, nor would they have believed the extent to which these frauds and outrages have been practiced, until they came to investigate them.

Mormon missionaries were always very active in Great Britain, bringing to the United States hundreds of their converts, who would then colonize an area in their preserve in Utah. This is an account of one such effort, led by Frederick Piercy.
(Source: Frederick Piercy, Route From Liverpool to Great Salt Lake Valley, Liverpool, 1855.)

After looking out and selecting a location, we formed our waggons into two parallel lines, some seventy paces apart. We then took our boxes from the wheels, and planted them about a couple of paces from each other, so securing ourselves that we could not easily be taken advantage of by any unknown foe. This done, we next cut a road up the Kanyon, opening it to a distance of some eight miles, bridging the creek in some five or six places, making the timber and poles (of which there is an immense quantity) of easy access. We next built a large meeting-house in the form of two rectangles, lying transversely, two stories high, of large pine trees, all well hewn and neatly jointed together. We next built a large square fort, with a commodious cattle carrel inside the inclosure. The houses built were some of hewn logs, and some of adobies, all neat, comfortable and convenient. We next inclosed a field some five by three miles square, with a good ditch and pole fence. We dug canals and water ditches to the distance of some 30 or 40 miles. One canal to turn the water of another creek upon the field, for irrigating purposes, was seven miles long. We built a saw and grist mill the same season. I have neither time nor space to tell you of one-half of the labours we performed here in one season. Suffice it to say that, when the Governor came along in the spring, he pronounced it the greatest work done in the mountains by the same amount of men . . . .

One of the most famous British emigrants to come to the United States in the 1860's was the English Jew, Samuel Gompers, who would become the long-time leader of the American Federation of Labor.   The motivation for his coming is described in his reminiscences.

(Source: Samuel Gompers, Seventy Years of Life and Labor, New York, 1925.)

It became harder and harder to get along as our family increased and expenses grew.   London seemed to offer no response to our efforts toward betterment.   About this time we began to hear more and more about the United States.   The great struggle against human slavery which was convulsing America was of vital interest to wage-earners who were everywhere struggling for industrial opportunity and freedom.   My work in the cigar factory gave me a chance to hear the men discuss this issue.   Youngster that I was, I was absorbed in listening to this talk and made my little contribution by singing with all the feeling in my little heart the popular songs, "The Slave Ship" and "To the West, To the West, To the Land of the Free."

It was typical of the feeling among English wage-earners of my boyhood days that the two most popular songs were "The Slave Ship" and "To the West."   I learned both and sang them with a fervor in which all my feeling quivered and throbbed.   I could throw back my head and sing:

> To the west, to the west, to the land of the free
> Where mighty Missouri rolls down to the sea;
> Where a man is a man if he's willing to toil,
> And the humblest may gather the fruits of the soil.
> Where children are blessings and he who hath most
> Has aid for his fortune and riches to boast.
> Where the young may exult and the aged may rest,
> Away, far away, to the land of the west.

The song expressed my feeling of America and my desire to go there rose with the ringing chorus:

> Away! far away, let us hope for the best
> And build up a home in the land of the west.

Years afterward Andrew Carnegie told me this song had inspired his father with a desire to come to America.

BIBLIOGRAPHY

The bibliography which follows, by no means exhausts the relatively large amount of sources concerned with British immigration to America, but does provide the reader with a good starting point to continue the study of this vital area of American immigration history. Remarkable as it may be, of all the various immigrant groups that came to the United States, the British have been written about most imperfectly, and as a result, any bibliography about them is scattered, and full of gaps. No really definitive history concerned with their movement to America, and their life in America has yet been undertaken. However, a number of good monographs have been published, and are included in the list that appears on the following pages.

This bibliography is divided into five sections; the English and Cornish, the Welsh, the Scotch, the Scotch-Irish, and British-American newspapers. Some of the works listed are quite old, but still contain valuable information. Space limitations have prevented the author from including a number of other references which are invaluable for the student pursuing research in this area. These, however, would include; Records of Immigrant Societies and Churches, British Diplomatic and Consular Correspondence, letters from immigrants to friends and relatives in the Old Country, Parliamentary, Congressional and State Documents, a host of immigrant guidebooks, general newspapers, trade-union newspapers, and other special periodicals of the time. One of the Most fruitful sections of this bibliography is the one dealing with British-American newspapers and journals. As most of these are long forgotten, this partial list gives their places, inclusive dates of publication, and libraries holding files.

A note about the Scotch-Irish bibliography section should be stated. While many Irish historians view the Scotch-Irish movement as an early part of the general Irish immigration of the nineteenth century, it is this author's opinion that the Scotch-Irish should be included within the category of British immigrants, as their characteristics seem more closely akin to the Scotch than the Irish during the period that their greatest influx to the American colonies took place.

Finally, references to the Irish and the British who entered the United States from Canada have been deliberately omitted, since their respective movements were so large and distinct that separate bibliographies concerned with these two groups can be compiled rather easily. Moreover, sources concerned with the colonial period of American history, which is essentially British-American history, have also been avoided for obvious reasons.

Allies, M. English Prelude. New York, 1936.

Bancroft, Caroline. "Cousin Jack Stories From Central City."
Colorado Magazine, XXI, 1944.

Banks, C. E. and Morison, S. E. "Persecution as a Factor in Emigration." Massachusetts Historical Society Proceedings. LXIII, 1930.

Berthoff, R. T. British Immigrants in Industrial America. Cambridge, Massachusetts, 1953. Probably the best single book on the subject, although it deals primarily with the nineteenth century.

Bestor, Arthur E. Backwoods Utopias. New York, 1950. Excellent volume on communitarian experiments in America.

Bridges, H. J. On Becoming an American. New York, 1919.

British Mechanic's and Laborer's Handbook and True Guide to the United States. London, 1842. A typical example of an emigrant guide book of the nineteenth century.

Byron, Thomas F. "The British-American Movement." American. XVI, 1888.

Cannon, M. Hamlin. "Migration of English Mormons to America." American Historical Review. LII, 1947.

----------------"The English Mormons in America." American Historical Review. LVII, 1952.

Carrothers, W. A. Emigration From the British Isles. London, 1929, A standard work on the subject.

Casson, Herbert N. "The English in America." Munsey's Magazine. XXXIV, 1906.

Copeland, Louis Albert. "The Cornish in Southwest Wisconsin." Collections of the State Historical Society of Wisconsin. XIV, 1898.

Crouse, Nellis M. "Causes of the Great Migration." New England Quarterly. V, 1932.

Cunliffe-Owen, F. "Englishmen in the United States." Forum. XXIX, 1900.

Erickson, Charlotte. "Agrarian Myths of English Immigrants," in Oscar F. Ander. In the Trek of the Immigrants. Rock Island, Illinois, 1964.

--------------------"Encouragement of Emigration by British Trade Unions." Population Studies. III, 1949.

Ettinger, A. A. James Edward Ogelthorpe. New York, 1936. Solid biography of the leading founder of Georgia.

Fisher, James. "Michigan's Cornish People." Michigan History Magazine. XXIX, 1945.

Flower, George. History of the English Settlement in Edwards County, Illinois. Chicago, 1882.

Foreman, Grant. "English Immigrants in Iowa." Iowa Journal of History and Politics. ILIV, 1946.

--------------------"English Settlers in Illinois." Journal of the Illinois State Historical Society. XXXIV, 1941.

Handlin, Oscar. Boston's Immigrants. Cambridge, Massachusetts, 1941. An outstanding work on the makeup of Boston's ethnic groups with especial emphasis on the Irish and British.

Hansen, Marcus L. The Mingling of the Canadian and American People. New Haven, 1940. Very good study on a difficult aspect of American immigration history.

Heaton, Herbert. "Yorkshire Cloth Traders in the United States, 1770-1840." Publications of the Thoresby Society. XXXVII, 1941.

Hitchins, Fred H. The Colonial Land and Emigration Commission. Philadelphia, 1931.

Horn, Harcourt. An English Colony in Iowa. Boston, 1931. Detailed study of one immigrant community. Very well done.

Hughes, Thomas. Rugby, Tennessee. London, 1881. Old, but still useful study of an English communitarian colony.

Irwin, Frederick T. The Story of Sandwich Glass. Manchester, New Hampshire, 1926.

Jenkin, A. K. Hamilton. The Cornish Miner. London, 1927.

Johnson, Stanley, A History of Emigration from the United Kingdom to North America, 1763-1912. London, 1913. An old, but valuable book dealing in comprehensive fashion with the subject.

Jones, Evan. The Emigrant's Friend. London, 1880. A typical and humorous guide book of the second half of the nineteenth century.

Larsen, Gustive O. "The Perpetual Emigrating Fund." Mississippi Valley Historical Review. XVIII, 1931.

Malone, Dumas. The Public Life of Thomas Cooper, 1783-1831. New York, 1936. Good Biography of the famous English immigrant politician.

Meserve, H. C. Lowell, An Industrial Dream Come True. Boston, 1923.

Moro, Arthur R. "The English Colony at Fairmount, Minnesota." Minnesota History. VIII, 1927.

Morrison, George A. A History of St. George's Society of New York. New York, 1913.

Newton, A. P. The Colonizing Activities of the English Puritans. New York, 1914.

Owen, Harold. The Staffordshire Potter. London, 1901.

Perrigo, Lynn I. "The Cornish Miners of Early Gilpin County." Colorado Magazine. XIV, 1937.

Pooley, William V. The Settlement of Illinois from 1830 to 1850. Madison, Wisconsin, 1908.

Quaife, Milo M. ed. An English Settler in Pioneer Wisconsin. Madison, Wisconsin, 1918. Very interesting diary of pioneer days in Wisconsin as told by an English immigrant.

Reports of the Select Committee on Emigration from the United Kingdom. various dated.

Reynolds, Lloyd G. The British Immigrant. Toronto, 1935.

Rodgers, T. History of Odd Fellowship. Paterson, New Jersey, 1925.

Rowse, A. L. The Cousin Jacks: The Cornish in America. New York, 1969.

Shepperson, W. S. British Emigration to North America: Projects and Opinions in the Early Victorian Period. Minneapolis, 1957. Exhaustive, well documented study of the statistical aspects of the subject.

-----------------Emigration and Disenchantment: Portraits of Englishmen Repatriated from the United States. Norman, Oklahoma, 1965.

Smith, E. F. Priestly in America, 1794-1804. New York, 1920. Semi-biographical study of the great English scientist and his years in the United States.

Spargo, John. "On Becoming an American Citizen." Independent, LXV, 1908.

------------------The Potters and Potteries of Bennington. Boston, 1924.

Spender, Harold. A Briton in America. London, 1921.

Stevenson, Robert Louis. The Amateur Immigrant. London, 1924. A classic book by the renowned British author.

Taylor, Philip A. M. "Why Did British Mormons Emigrate?" Utah Historical Quarterly. XXII, 1954.

Thomas, B. Migration and Economic Growth: A Study of Great Britain and the Atlantic Economy. Cambridge, 1954. Penetrating study of the economic aspects of the immigration question in Great Britain.

Walpole, Kathleen A. Emigration to British North America under the Early Navigation Acts. Unpublished M. A. Thesis, London, 1929.

Webb, Robert K. "Working Class Readers in Early Victorian England." English Historical Review. LXV, 1950.

White, G. S. Memoirs of Samuel Slater, the Father of American Manufactures. Boston, 136. Dated, but still contains very valuable information of the early textile industry and those British immigrants who formed the core of its early workers.

Wister, William R. Some Reminiscences of Cricket in Philadelphia before 1861. Philadelphia, 1904.

Yearly, Clifford K. Britons in American Labor. Baltimore, 1957, Very good study, up to date, and well documented.

Zee, Jacob van der. The British in Iowa. Iowa City, Iowa, 1922.

WELSH

Abrams, J. L. "The Welsh People of Irontown." Cambrian, I, 1880-1881.

Blackwell, Henry. "A Bibliography of Welsh Americana." National Library of Wales Journal. Supplement, 1942. Indispensable tool in studying the subject. Needs to be updated.

Brierley, Benjamin. Ab-O'th-Yate in Yankeeland. Manchester, 1885.

Brower, Edith. "The Meaning of an Eisteddfod." Atlantic. LXXV, 1895. Colorful, amusing article on an important aspect of Welsh life in America.

Browning, C. H. Welsh Settlements in Pennsylvania. Philadelphia, 1912.

Casson, H. N. "Welsh in America." Munsey's Magazine. XXXIV, 1906.

Conway, Alan. The Welsh in America. Cardiff, 1961, Very good, up to date study of the Welsh immigrant in the United States based upon various immigrant letters.

Darlington, Thomas. "The Welsh in America." Wales. I, 1894.

Davies, Howell. History of the Oskosh Welsh Settlement. Amarillo, 1947.

Davis, J. F. The Iron Puddler. Indianapolis, 1922.

Ebbutt, Percy G. Emigrant Life in Kansas. London, 1886. Old, but interesting work, written from Welsh immigrant's point of view.

Edwards, Ebenezer. Welshmen as Factors. Utica, New York, 1899.

Evans, Chris. History of the United Mineworkers of America. Indianapolis, 1919. Though old, an excellent study of the origins and early problems of this organization.

Evans, Paul De Mund. The Welsh in Oneida County. Ithaca, New York, 1914.

Glen, T. A. Welsh Founders of Pennsylvania. London, 1932. Comprehensive, well done work on the colonial Welsh immigrants.

Hartmann, Edward G. Americans From Wales. Boston, 1967. Modern up-to-date study. Scholarly and perceptive; Well documented with good bibliography.

Hughes, David. The Welsh People of California, 1849-1906. San Francisco, 1923.

Hughes, Thomas. History of the Welsh in Minnesota. Mankato, 1895.

Husband, Joseph. A Year in a Coal Mine. Boston, 1911. A vivid description of Welsh coal miners, and mining procedures.

Jones, David. Welsh Congregationalists in Pennsylvania. Utica, New York, 1934.

Jones, E. W. "The Welsh in America." Atlantic Monthly. March, 1876.

Jones, William Harvey. "Welsh Settlements in Ohio." Ohio Archeological and Historical Quarterly. XVI, 1907.

Lewis, Idwal. "Welsh Newspapers and Journals in the United States." National Library of Wales Journal. II, 1942.

Monaghan, Jay. "The Welsh People in Chicago." Journal of the Illinois State Historical Society. XXXII, 1939. Excellent short study of the Welsh immigrant in an urban environment.

Morgan, W. P. "The Welsh in the United States." Wales. III, 1896.

Morgan, Vyrnwy. The Cambro-American Pulpit. New York, 1898. Though old, this is a detailed study of the development of the Welsh church in the United States. Still valuable.

Owen, "Welsh American Newspapers and Periodicals." National Library of Wales Journal. VI, 1950.

Rhys, H. S. The Welsh People. New York, 1923. Valuable general history of the people of Wales. Good starting point for the whole subject of Welsh immigration.

Spencer, J. Denley. "Young Welshmen Abroad." Wales. IV, 1897.

Schaefer, Joseph. The Wisconsin Lead Region. Madison, Wisconsin, 1932.

Thomas, Howard. "The Welsh Came to Remsen." New York History. XXX, 1949.

Thomas, Robert D. Hanes Cymry America. Utica, New York, 1872.

Tyler, L. G. The Cradle of the Republic. Richmond, 1906. Old, but still useful work on the early Welsh immigrant's role in the American Revolution.

Williams, Daniel J. The Welsh of Columbus, Ohio. Oshkosh, 1913. Good local history of the Welsh immigrant group.

------------------The Welsh Community of Waukesha County. Columbus, Ohio, 1926.

-----------------One Hundred Years of Welsh Calvinistic Methodism in
America. Philadelphia, 1937.

SCOTCH

Babson, R. W. W. B. Wilson. New York, 1919. Very good biography of
the famous Scottish immigrant and his contributions to American life
and society.

Bradley, A. G. "Ulster Scot in the United States." Nineteenth Century.
LXXI, 1912.

Black, George F. Scotland's Mark on America. New York, 1921.
Rather superficial treatment of Scottish immigrant contributions to the
United States.

Casson, H. N. "The Son of the Old Scotland in America." Munsey's
Magazine. XXXIV, 1906.

Crockett, A. S. When James Gordon Bennett was Caliph of Bagdad.
New York, 1926. Popular biography of the famed Scottish immigrant who
became an outstanding newspaper publisher in New York.

Dunn, Charles W. Highland Settler. Toronto, 1953. Modern, well
written study of those Highland Scots who came to America.

Graham, Ian C. C. Colonists From Scotland: Emigration to North
America, 1707-1783. New York, 1956.

Harvey, Daniel G. The Argyle Settlement in History and Story. Rock-
ford, Illinois, 1924.

Hendrick, Burton J. The Life of Andrew Carnegie. 2 vols. New York,
1932. Probably the best biography on the great Scotch industrialist.

Higginson, Thomas W. "A Day of Scottish Games." Scribner's III,
1872.

Irvine, A. Bain., ed. The Scots Year Book. London, 1927.

Johnston, David. Reminiscences of an Octagenarian Scotsman. Chicago,
1885.

Mac Donald, R. H. The Emigration of Highland Crofters. Edinburgh,
1885.

Mac Dougall, David, ed. Scots and Scots Descendents in America. New
York, 1917. Though old, still valuable as a listing of early Scottish immigrants and their descendents.

----------------, ed. The American Year Book-Directory of Scottish Societies and British Associations in the United States, Canada, and British Possessions. New York, 1914.

Mac Kenzie, C. D. Alexander Graham Bell. Boston, 1928. Good biography of the inventor of the telephone.

Mac Lean, J. P. An Historical Account of the Settlement of the Scotch-Highlanders in America to 1783. Cleveland, 1900. Old, but contains much valuable information.

Mac Millan, Thomas C. "The Scots and their descendents in Illinois." Transactions of the Illinois State Historical Society. 1919.

Morrison, George A. History of the St. Andrew's Society of Charleston, South Carolina. Charleston, 1929.

----------------.History of the St. Andrew's Society of the State of New York. New York, 1906.

Murdock, Angus. Boom Copper. New York, 1943. Excellent study of the development of western copper mines by Scottish immigrant mines.

Murray, J. S. "Lairds of North Tama." Iowa Journal of History and Politics. XL, 1942.

Rahill, F. "National Origins in Pennsylvania." Commonweal. X, 1929.

Reid, W. The Scot in America. London, 1911. Out-dated, but interesting work. Still valuable for factual material.

Todd, William. The Seventy-Ninth Highlanders. Albany, 1886. Though old, very good work on the famed Scottish Civil War regiment.

Wilson, M. The Able McLaughlin's. New York, 1923.

SCOTCH-IRISH

Baldwin, Leland D. The Whiskey Rebels: The Story of a Frontier Uprising. Pittsburgh, 1939. Excellent study of the late nineteenth century incident and the part played in it by the Scotch-Irish frontiersmen.

Barton, Thomas. The Conduct of the Paxton Men, Impartially Considered. Philadelphia, 1764. Very old, but interesting study by a contemporary of the "Paxton Boys" in Pennsylvania.

Bassett, J. S. The Regulators of North Carolina. Washington, D. C., 1895.

Bolton, C. K. Scotch-Irish Pioneers in Ulster and America. Boston, 1910.

Briggs, C. A. American Presbyterianism: Its Origins and History. New York, 1885.

Chalkley, Lyman. Chronicles of the Scotch-Irish Settlement in Virginia, Extracted from the Original Court Records of Augusta County, 1745-1800. 3 vols. Rosslyn, Virginia, 1912.

Christian, Bolivar. The Scotch-Irish in the Valley of Virginia. Richmond, 1860.

Coolidge, R. D. "Scotch-Irish in New England." New England Magazine. XLII, 1910.

Demond, Robert O. The Loyalists in North Carolina During the Revolution. Durham, North Carolina. 1944.

Dinsmore, John W. The Scotch-Irish in America. Chicago, 1906.

Dunaway, Wayland F. The Scotch-Irish of Colonial Pennsylvania. Philadelphia, 1944. Excellent, detailed study of the Scotch-Irish movement into Pennsylvania.

Finley, John, H. The Coming of the Scot. New York, 1940.

Ford, H. J. The Scotch-Irish in America. Princeton, New Jersey, 1915. Although old, this work remains the classic study of the Scotch-Irish in the United States.

Garland, Robert. The Scotch-Irish in Western Pennsylvania. Pittsburgh, 1923.

Glasgow, M. The Scotch-Irish in Northern Ireland, and in the American Colonies. New York, 1936.

Green, Edward R. R. "The Scotch-Irish and the Coming of the Revolution in North Carolina." Irish Historical Studies. VII, 1950.

Green, Samuel S. The Scotch-Irish in America. Worcester, Massachusetts, 1895.

Hoyt, W. M. The Mecklenburg Declaration of Independence. New York, 1907. Very interesting, if old, work on a relatively little known aspect of American history.

Klett, Guy S. The Scotch-Irish in Pennsylvania. Gettysburg, 1948.

Leyburn, James G. The Scotch-Irish. Chapel Hill, North Carolina, 1962. Excellent, well documented, up-to-date study on the Scotch-Irish in Britain, Ireland, and America.

Mebane, C. H., ed. The Scotch Irish Settlements. Raleigh, North Carolina, 1908.

Meyers, A. C. Immigration of the Irish Quakers into Pennsylvania, 1682-1750. Philadelphia, 1902.

O'Connell, J. D. The Scotch-Irish Delusion in America. Washington, D. C., 1897.

Perry, Arthur L. "The-Scotch-Irish in New England." Proceedings and Addresses of the Scotch-Irish Society of America. II. Nashville, 1890-1900.

Reid, Whitelaw. The Scot in America and the Ulster Scot. London, 1912.

Ross, Peter. The Scot in America. New York, 1896.

Wertenbaker, T. J. Early Scotch Contributions to the United States. Glasgow, 1945. Scholarly treatment of the subject.

Albion, New York, 1822-1876, Boston Athenceum.

Anglo-American, London, 1898-? 1898-1902. British Museum.

Anglo-American Magazine, New York, 1899-1902. New York, Public Library.

Boston Scotsman, Boston, 1906-1914. Order of Scottish Clans, Boston.

British-American, New York, Philadelphia, 1887-1919. British Museum.

British-American Citizen, Boston, 1887-1913. Massachusetts Historical Society; Huntington Library.

British Californian, San Francisco, 1897-1931. Library of Congress, New York Public Library.

Cambrian, Cincinnati, Utica, 183-1934. Harvard University Library, Library of Congress; New York Public Library.

Cenhadur Americanaidd, Utica, 1883-1934. Harvard University Library, Library of Congress; New York Public Library.

Cenhadur Americanaidd, Utica, Remsen, 1840-1901. National Library of Wales.

Cyfaill o'r Hen Wlad, New York, Utica, 1838-1933. National Library of Wales.

Cymro America, New York, 1832. Nwional Library of Wales.

Druid (Welsh-American), Scranton, Pittsburgh, 1907-1939. National Library of Wales; Welsh National Library of North America.

Drych, New York, Utica, 1851--- . National Library of Wales; University College of North Wales Library; Harvard University Library; Harvard University Library.

Emigrant, New York, 1833-1835. Library of Congress.

Emigrant and Old Countryman, New York, 1835-1840. Library of Congress; American Antiquarian Society.

English-American, New York, 1884-1885. British Museum.

English-Speaking World, New York, 1917-1922. New York Public Library.

Fiery Cross, Boston, 1900-1950. Order of Scottish Clans, Boston.

New York Anglo-American, New York, 1843-1846. New York Public Library; Library of Congress.

Old Countryman, New York, 1842-1848. Library of Congress.

Scottish-American, New York, 1857, 1919. Chicago Historical Society; New York Public Library; Boston Public Library; New York Historical Society.

Scottish Patriot, New York, 1840-1842. New York Historical Society.

INDEX

Waldo, Samuel, 15
Weaver, Daniel, 41
Wentworth, Benning, 11
West, George, 44
Wheelwright, John, 7
White, John, 1,2
William and Mary, 12
Williams, Roger, 7
Wilson, James, 23

Wilson, Woodrow, 29
Winthrop, John, 5,6,7
Winthrop, John Jr., 7
Witherspoon, John, 20,23
Wyatt, Francis, 5
Wyncop, John, 3

Yeardley, George, 3